THE OFFICIAL

ROCK PAPER SCISSORS

STRATEGY GUIDE

DOUGLAS WALKER
GRAHAM WALKER

ILLUSTRATIONS BY MEGAN BANNON

A FIRESIDE BOOK
PUBLISHED BY SIMON & SCHUSTER

NEW YORK   LONDON   TORONTO   SYDNEY

FIRESIDE
Rockefeller Center
1230 Avenue of the Americas
New York, NY 10020

Designed by Ruth Lee-Mui

For information regarding special discounts for bulk purchases,
please contact Simon & Schuster Special Sales at 1-800-456-6798
or business@simonandschuster.com

Manufactured in the United States of America

10   9   8   7   6   5   4   3   2   1

ISBN 0-7432-6751-6

TO LISA, FOR ALL HER HARD WORK
AND DEDICATION THAT IS
RARELY RECOGNIZED

CONTENTS

Rock Paper Scissors— Game or Sport?

Master Roshambollah

Other than the obscure origins of Rock Paper Scissors (or RPS) and such imponderables as how Paper beats Rock, perhaps no other issue has so captivated the attention of the public as this one: Namely, is RPS by nature more of a game or more of a sport? Truly it can be called either, but which is the best descriptor for our beloved pastime? This issue continues to divide the community as a whole, and there is no sign of the debate dying down. With interest in RPS at an all-time high, a new perspective has never been needed more.

Perhaps some introductions and qualifications are in order. My name is Master Roshambollah, and I am considered by some to be the best professional RPS player in the world. I have played—and won—RPS matches on three different continents. If it's a major tournament I've competed in it, from the Southwest US ProAms and the Northeast Classic to the vaunted International Championship itself. There is perhaps no other person more qualified to approach this question from a player's perspective.

No one debates whether or not **RPS** is a game. Indeed, it may be the world's oldest strategy game. It is certainly the most basic; three is the minimum number of elements needed for an interesting strategy game (with two elements, one will always dominate). The game's best players obsessively watch videos of their opponents, keep up on the latest game theory, and study the great games of past masters. In this manner, we develop the mental qualities needed to succeed. In the classic work *Trio of Hands,* renowned **RPS** grandmaster Wojek Smallsoa calls **RPS** "the game of kings and paupers, of athletes and scholars, of warriors and peacemakers." As a game, **RPS** is used today by millions of people all over the world as a means of solving disputes great and small— from territorial disputes to deciding who has to take out the garbage.

But is RPS a sport as well? To answer this question, we must identify the difference between the two concepts. Games and sports share the element of competition; in this sense, checkers is just as much of a "game" as basketball. The key difference is the nature of the competition. With lesser strategy games such as tic-tac-toe, dominoes, or chess, the nature of competition is merely mental. With sports such as boxing, football, or golf, the competition takes on a physical aspect as well. And it is for this reason we must also consider RPS a sport.

No one who has seen the masters of RPS compete can doubt that the game involves both physical and mental efforts of the highest level. However, the great players always have their game rooted in the physical, in the seemingly effortless victories they achieve with throw after throw. The degree of physical involvement takes on new dimensions at the highest levels of the sport. Like all professional athletes, RPS players train heavily for major tournaments, making use of weight lifting and stretching exercises. Among professional players, physical injuries are all too common, ranging from repetitive-motion injuries to "knuckle dusting" (direct fist-to-fist contact).

To me, RPS is both game and sport, as well as a way of life. The cycle of life on Earth forms a pattern. Water evaporates from the ocean, becomes rain, then flows in rivers back to the ocean. Plants and animals breathe carbon dioxide and oxygen in the air in an endless exchange, each producing what the other needs. Earth spins on its axis and revolves around the sun so that season follows season in predictable order. Consider the rise and fall of civilizations and the patterns of birth, life, and death. Every beginning is an end, and every end is a beginning. So it is with RPS; one throw beats another, only to be defeated in turn by the third. RPS is a cycle as well. Thus, life is a reflection of Rock Paper Scissors.

• • •

Although the discussion will no doubt continue, the future of the sport is not in question. And whether you view RPS as game or sport, you now hold in your hands a strategic guidebook that will allow you to take your game to the next level. This work is not intended to replace the voluminous *Standard Openings*, which exhaustively explores the almost sixty thousand possible permutations of a typical five-throw opening series between two players. It should also not be compared to the gentle poetry of Smallsoa's *Trio of Hands*. This book is intended to level the playing field, to provide the newcomer with the strategic skills needed to meet more advanced players on their own terms. The RPS masters, in turn, will be forced to further improve their own strategies, which can only be good for the game's future.

By reading this book, you will learn basic rules of RPS, fundamentals such as gambit play, and even more advanced strategies. You will learn these secrets from the two individuals most qualified to teach them: Douglas and Graham Walker. The Walker brothers have done much to return RPS to the days of its greatest glory. Under the direction of the World Rock Paper Scissors Society, they organize the annual International Championships of the sport. Through the society's Web site, sanctioned tournaments, and published works, they have succeeded in encouraging fair play, sound strategy, and strong throws. The Walkers are also excellent RPS players (though not quite masters). Graham and Douglas have once again served the future of the sport and the champions of tomorrow by committing the highest ideals of play to this tome. It is a great honor to introduce to you this invaluable guide.

A History of Rock Paper Scissors

"It is not the tongue of man that will
abolish conflict, but the hand."

Lincoln Waderham, first Steering Committee
chairman of the Paper Scissors Stone Club, 1842

Because Rock Paper Scissors, a game played primarily with one's mind and hands, leaves little tangible evidence, historians and anthropologists have left the game's historical roots and cultural significance largely unexplored. However, a wealth of knowledge from written accounts and oral traditions gives us some tantalizing clues into the early history of the game. Project Dig It, commissioned by the World RPS Society, has scoured hundreds of ongoing archaeological sites around the world searching for clues. Though researchers have unearthed the bones of countless hands in poses resembling the RPS hand formations, there has been no conclusive proof that can link those skeletal remains with the game of Rock Paper Scissors.

What we do know has been distilled here.

EARLY FORMS OF HAND GAMES

While Rock Paper Scissors is certainly the most elegant and profound of all conflict-resolution processes, it is not the original. The first known proto-RPS game was played widely by early Homo sapiens circa 50,000 B.C. and was used primarily to resolve food and mating disputes. The game involved only one hand position almost identical to a modern-day throw of Rock. The game would involve two or more players, with some players acting as "throwers" and the others as "catchers." The thrower would attempt to place his Rock at a strategic position on another player's body; the catcher would then attempt to avoid the opponent's throw. The players would frequently reverse positions until one player successfully placed an unspecified number of Rocks upon his opponent. Even today the game remains inexplicably popular, particularly wherever alcohol is served. It has been reported that in modern times the game will eschew the use of hands entirely in favor of environmental objects such as chairs and bottles.

Over the centuries this game was further advanced to include the use of open hands to stop or block a throw of Rock and also began to use the index and middle fingers (or the "eye-poker" as it was then known). It was this very early form of RPS that was the inspiration for martial arts throughout India, China, Korea, and Japan. The martial arts, however, went much further in terms of developing new throws, and even took it to the unnecessary extreme of using feet. The game quickly became a parody of itself. Subsequently, many players who were alienated from the pointless violence of the game took divine inspiration from the most unsavory of places—two reptiles and a slug.

JANKEN, OR THE BIRTH OF MODERN RPS

Janken, as the first known true RPS game, was roused into existence by application of the Guu Choki Paa (or Sansukumi) way of thinking, which can be defined as a nontransitive tripartite system, or, in laymen's terms, a three-way impasse. Guu Choki Paa describes how the snake fears the slug; the slug fears the frog; and the frog fears the snake. When all three are present, they are held in balance so that none can triumph over another. When only two are present the balance is disrupted, allowing one to dominate over another. The associations between Rock, Paper, and Scissors, or, as some call it, the "trinity," is described accurately, albeit distastefully by the Guu Choki Paa system.

The notion of a nonviolent conflict-resolution method held in blissful balance by such an elegant trio of throws was certainly among the greatest achievements of Oriental culture. However, Snake, Slug, and Frog did not gain the widespread appeal that its creators had intended, particularly among the fairer sex. Participants and creators alike agreed that the elements used in the game were the root of the issue. So the search was on for three replacement elements that could be held in perfect balance, but would not make women squeamish. This search would last for generations.

In Japan, a new variant known as Tiger, Warrior, and Warrior's Mother emerged. The Tiger would devour the Warrior's Mother; the Warrior would best the Tiger; and the Warrior's Mother ruled over her Warrior son. While this formation held a certain charm, learning the extremely painful and contorted hand symbols required years of study. The renaissance was rather brief for all but a few masters of the discipline. The age of the Tiwawamo master was born.

"Tiwawamo" masters could spend many years of devoted study perfecting their craft. Local villages would call on them to help solve important disputes. A strong

Two Tiwawamo masters engaged in a highly ritualized version of RPS.

code of ethics bound the practitioners to acting only when both parties agreed to abide and honor the outcome. The highly ritualized event required many days of physical labor to create an arena worthy of the great masters of dispute resolution. So only matters of the highest priority for the villagers would be determined with this system. Due to the rigors of training and the extended ritual involved, the game never gained renown and was eventually abandoned.

As an enterprising young trader exploring the eastern regions, Marco Polo brought back not only tales of Oriental splendor but also stories of the use of a truly inspired dispute-resolution mechanism (this critical detail has been omitted by all known scholarly works on the man). The traders of Venice took the Tiwawamo system and quickly adapted the simpler Rock Paper Scissors variation to capitalize on its potential uses to settle frequent trade disputes.

Many scholars believe that the game Polo brought back was actually a version known as Rock Paper Blade, and that the Venetians simply substituted the "blade" with their own invention, the "scissors." Eastern scholars, however, claim that the shift from Tiwawamo to the Rock, Paper, and Blade symbols happened during the transition of the game between Japan and Kublai Chan's China, where Marco Polo discovered the practice. No matter what the true story, careful analysis of the symbols gives us an exciting clue into the modern version of the sport.

The origin of rock on Earth dates back to approximately 4.5 billion B.C. Papyrus (early paper) was developed during ancient Egyptian times. So it is the invention of the scissors that gives us the earliest possible date for the game of RPS. Scissors were invented in the year 500 A.D. by a hair cutter, named Isidore of Seville, Italy. This vital discovery has revealed the existence of an RPS dark age lasting over a thousand years between the evolution of Janken in Japan and the invention of the scissors. In an attempt to pinpoint the origin of the game more precisely, the World RPS Society commissioned the ORiGIN (Official Research into Game-development from Independent Nations) Task Force to investigate cross-cultural references and shine light upon the mystery.

World RPS Society ORiGIN Task Force

The most intriguing conclusion from the ORiGIN report, other than the astonishing number of names for the game, was that each culture studied appears to lay claim to having invented RPS. The World RPS Society's on-staff actuaries and logicians have assured us that the odds of more than two cultures developing the game independently, with all of its dizzying complexity, approaches zero. The debatable issue of which culture actually "invented" the game has been widely considered to be the underlying cause for several of today's most heated national rivalries on the World RPS Pro circuit.

The World RPS Society ORiGIN Task Force's report, released in 1996, stated, "There is no doubt through the evidence gathered by this task force that the game of Rock, Paper, Scissors was independently invented in both Eastern Europe and Japan." It came as an incredible shock that the task force had ruled out Italy as the European root. "The evidence is overwhelming, conclusive, and inarguable," continued the report. This finding immediately came into question when the Italian National RPS Chapter demanded a review. The review process, under the watchful eye of the steering committee, was a painstaking investigation into all of the source material used by the task force. After the review was nearly abandoned due to an inability to find several of the "secret" or "damaged" documents referred to in the report, an enterprising young secretary named Rose O'Dell closely examined the task force roster and revealed in a memo to Chairman Smallsoa that "the entire complement of the task force appears to be of immediate Oriental or Czech descent." The ORiGIN report was subsequently discredited by the steering committee, and the Italian theory was once again on firm footing. For her service to the society, Ms. O'Dell was to receive the title "Morale Officer." However, due to a clerical error, she became the "Moral Officer" and ever since has imposed her own unique style of ethics upon the World RPS Society.

Other theories of the game's appearance in Europe come to us from France. In the mid-1700s, when trade began to accelerate between Europe and the Orient, the game likely migrated into France along with the trading expeditions. The game eventually became synonymous with a military commander by the name of Jean Baptiste Donatien de Vimeur, who also held the title of le Comte de Rochambeau (1725–1807). It is widely believed that an ill-advised throw of Scissors (or Ciseaux) resulted in his being uprooted from his ancestral home to become the marshal of the French forces during the American Revolution. His arrival is widely credited with the introduction of RPS to the United States.

HISTORY OF THE
WORLD ROCK PAPER SCISSORS SOCIETY

The Paper Scissors Stone Club was the first club of its kind dedicated to the finest of all dispute-resolution methodologies. It was founded in London, England, in 1842 as a result of a highly controversial law issued that same year that declared, "Any decision reached by the use of the process known as Paper Scissors Stone between two gentlemen acting in good faith shall constitute a binding contract. Agreements reached in this manner are subject to all relevant contract and tort law." While on the surface this law simply legalized the well-established practice of firm adherence to decisions arrived at this way, the greater concern was the subsequent enforcement. For many constables the law was interpreted to mean that the game could not be played simply for sport. So when playing on the street, individuals would frequently be interrupted by police, with a hearty "What's all this then?" The recreational players were then forced to create arbitrary decisions out of thin air. During the frequent enforcement crackdowns, the state of affairs could be so disrupted that sporting players often kept long lists of prescripted decisions in their coat pockets in case their games were prematurely ended by London bobbies.

"What's all this then?" A constable interrupts an RPS match in typical fashion at the time.

WOJEK SMALLSOA ON RPS DECISION MAKING

Many people go through their daily lives without paying due regard to one of the essential underpinnings of civilized life: the ability to resolve conflict without resorting to barbarism. The pinnacle of dispute resolution was achieved with the development of Rock Paper Scissors. The World Rock Paper Scissors Society has maintained this fine tradition of nonviolence since it was established in 1842. The essence of RPS is deeply rooted in dispute resolution. Together with its precursors, the sport has arrested arguments, dictated priorities, and condemned victims to undesired ends for centuries. There can be no question that, were it not for Rock Paper Scissors, the world would be a more brutal and distinctly less civilized place.

While the proponents (I hesitate to refer to their breed as "colleagues") of other conflict-resolution methodologies such as the Coin-Tossing Confederation; the Drawers of Straw; or the One

Potato, Two Potato League may claim similar violence-abating systems, one cannot help but pity these aficionados' dogged resolve to defend such infantile amusements. The supporters of these games prefer to hide behind the skirt of fickle chance when faced with a difficult decision, rather than facing the full brunt of their opponent's intellect and will, as do players of RPS.

The infuriating attitude of the police force was seen as a slap in the face to the growing number of enthusiasts who played the game strictly as a recreational activity. Thus, later that same year, the Paper Scissors Stone Club was founded and officially registered to provide a private environment, free from the long arm of the law, where enthusiasts could meet and play for honor. Honor points would be won and lost by players during the matches held in the now legendary Paper, Scissors, and Stone pub. The pub was on the main floor of the PSS Club headquarters and is often erroneously believed to be the origin of the partnership between RPS and alcohol.

The original charter appeared as the feature article of Edition 1, Volume 1, of *The Stone Scissors Paper*, which was published later the same year:

The club is dedicated to the exploration and dissemination of knowledge regarding the game of Paper Scissors Stone and providing a safe and legal environment for the playing of said game. We, the members, take it upon ourselves to educate others regarding the rules, customs, and etiquette of the game. Through the authority given to the Steering Committee by the membership, we shall also act as the overseeing body of all tournaments. Furthermore, we shall make every effort to protect the purity of the game from those who would wish to alter it.

—A bronze plaque weighing over two thousand pounds
and bearing these words still hangs prominently
in the Steering Committee chamber

In 1918, the name was changed to World RPS Club for two reasons: first, "world" was added to reflect the growing international membership base; and second, PSS was changed to RPS because of an offensive acronym that had come into popular usage. Detractors frequently used the term "PiSSers" to denote Paper Scissors Stone players. This term is widely suspected to have originated with members of the Coin-Tossing Confederation, who blamed the PSS Club for their entertaining and accurate appellation of "Tossers."

At roughly the same time, the club moved its headquarters from London to its present location at Trinity Square Plaza in Toronto, Canada. Despite an allied victory in World War I, the official reason for the move was outlined in the Annual World RPS Club chairman's address: "England is far too dangerous a place to make a

suitable home country for a game of conflict resolution."
Canada was seen as an excellent choice since it was seen
as a "safe, hospitable, and utterly inoffensive nation, a
part of the commonwealth, yet not inhabited by the de-
scendants of criminals."

RPS PLAYERS RESPONSIBILITY CODE

1. Safety first! Always ensure that all players have removed sharp
   jewelry and watches.
2. Ensure agreement, before the first round, on priming conventions (we recommend the standard three-prime shoot).
3. Always establish what is to be decided or whether the match is to
   be played for honor.
4. Predetermine the number of rounds required to win the match
   (remember odd numbers only).
5. Encourage novice development by explaining blunders in judgment with a mind toward being helpful. Don't berate.
6. Think twice before using RPS for life-threatening decisions.
7. Always respect foreign cultures. When abroad, consider yourself
   an ambassador of the World RPS Society.

In 1925, the name was changed to the World RPS Society once the club briefly reached more than 10,000 active members. The Steering Committee felt that because
the membership had reached a new order of magnitude
the term "club" was too inclusive. The first annual RPS
championship was also held in 1925.

The World RPS Society, like many organizations,
struggled during the Depression. With the majority of

enthusiasts searching for work and former world champions now passing the time playing RPS in soup lines, attendance at tournaments and membership dues dropped sharply. The formerly opulent surroundings of Trinity Square Plaza fell into disrepair. Before long the once great World RPS Society had become a quaint relic of a time long gone. The society seemed in danger of disappearing altogether, despite a few brief flare-ups of interest during the 1950s and '60s, particularly among left-wing beatniks and later hippies. This began the World RPS Society's use of socialist and Cultural Revolution imagery. Ryan Wollard of the Artistic Affairs Committee believes that socialists were drawn to the egalitarian and nonviolent nature of RPS as a decision-making mechanism. During this time, only a few members and society staff worked quietly and tirelessly perfecting strategies and gambits, and sharing their arcane knowledge among one another.

REBIRTH OF THE SOCIETY

By this time the World RPS Society had fallen on difficult times. Long gone were the heady times during the 1920s when an RPS champion would be honored by parades (though never via a ticker-tape parade, as was the custom at the time, due to the obvious throw bias). The glory of the society had been reduced to little more than a loose collection of drinking companions with a common interest. The active membership had fallen into single digits, and the World Championship of Rock Paper Scissors had not been held for years. Society lore has it that the lowest point came at a previous championship match. It was a ramshackle affair between a few grizzled RPS adversaries who met at a small pub to play for the World Championship title and a total prize purse of another round of bourbon. The only media in attendance was the bartender, who was reported to have announced the winner on the chalkboard behind the bar.

It was not until the winter of 1995 that the sport took a leap several minutes into the future, with the development of the first Web site dedicated to the sport: world rps.com. The gravity of the Web site quickly swept up any latent RPS activity and became the hub for enthusiasts from around the world. The bulletin board (or Bull Board) membership list became a who's who of the world's top players. A mere eighteen months later, in early 1997, the course of the society had been recharted away from its insular focus, and its teachings were finally available to the masses via the Web.

In 2002, the most important phase of the revitalization campaign began: rebuilding the World Championships. Breaking with tradition, the society established the first-ever open tournament. The public and media response was overwhelming and resulted in a sold-out venue and worldwide media coverage on the rebirth of the sport. With the success of the World Championship event, the World RPS Society had finally rekindled the world's interest in RPS, both as a dispute resolution method and a competitive sport.

Team UK 2003 *(left to right):* Dougal Kerr, James Lawson, Will Blackwell, and Andy Cumming. (Photo by Jon Lappin)

HOW TO PLAY

"Rock beats Scissors,
Scissors beats Paper, Paper beats Rock.
Some say that is how the game ends;
I say that is only where it begins."

Dennis "Finnegan" Tyler, player, 1956–65

WHY PLAY RPS?

As a game between two opponents, RPS, or the "Dance of Hands," has no equal. It sublimates the raw into the refined, requires no setup or equipment other than the functioning hands of two players, needs minimal communication, and can be played in any location. But, before one can answer the question of how to play RPS, it is important to ask *why* play RPS. Take a look at the following definition:

> "RPS is a decision-making vehicle that replaces the elements of Rock, Paper, and Scissors with three hand symbols that are thrown simultaneously by two players."
> —"RPS Player Guidelines" pamphlet, 1925

The core idea here is that RPS is by definition a "decision-making vehicle" rather than a game enjoyed simply for sport. While this does not mean that RPS cannot be enjoyed as a game, the dramatic decision-making properties are what give RPS its unique and characteristic flavor.

Many opponents to the RPS system ask, "Wouldn't it just be simpler to toss a coin?" On the surface it may appear so, but even a cursory look at coin tossing shows us otherwise. First, those who favor a coin toss as a dispute-resolution mechanism are dramatically different in character from RPS players, who tend to be more active rather than passively accepting the hand of fate. Second, coin tossers fail to acknowledge that the very fact that their game necessitates the use of a coin is often problematic:

Consider the following example:

Benji: Let's toss a coin for it.

Owen: Okay. I don't have any money though.

Benji: (digs through pockets) Found one!

Owen: That's too small. Don't you have anything bigger?

Benji: (digging again through pockets) Well, how 'bout this? (finds a larger coin)

Owen: That's fine. Now this coin doesn't have a "heads," so we'll make this side heads. (points to odd design)

Benji: Okay, fine. Now, you got to throw it last time, so this time I will be the thrower.

Owen: No, I want to throw it. You have trouble catching it in the air.

Benji: Fine, I will let it fall this time. Okay, call it! (flips the coin in the air)

Owen: Heads!

Benji: You called heads too late. It had already hit the ground. You have to call it in the air!

Owen: Uh-oh, the coin just rolled under the couch. Do you have another coin?

Benji: Just this small one.

Contrast this with the following

Benji: Let's RPS for it.

Owen: Okay. One, two, three, shoot . . .

[Benji throws Paper; Owen throws Scissors.]

Benji: Well played. You won.

The story above illustrates that coin tossing is actually *not* easier to instigate than RPS, quite the contrary. Also, notice in the latter example how Benji compliments Owen after the win? The lesson we learn here is that RPS games are won and lost as a direct result of how well one plays against the opponent. Losing a coin toss is a frustrating experience at best, because it often leaves a player feeling that fate has been unkind. There is no hand of fate in RPS. The ability to win or lose is based on physical and mental capabilities. Agreeing to toss a coin declares a preference to have fate make decisions than to be actively involved in the process. This may be fine in situations where neither decision maker cares about the outcome, but RPS players tend to have a vested interest in the outcome. They need only ask themselves if they are simply passive observers of their environment or active participants.

GAME BASICS

Most players learn to play RPS at a very young age, and while this has been an advantage in popularizing the game, it is also a breeding ground for bad habits. Game rules have been passed down from brother to sister, sister to neighbor, and neighbor to hairstylist, leaving many opportunities for slight variations and changes. The last thing that a decision-making methodology needs is confusion over the rules and practice of the game, but with so many regional and local variations, it can require a lengthy negotiation simply to arrive at the basics. For those interested in high-level competition, the Official Rules of the Grand Sport of Rock Paper Scissors can be found in Appendix 1; however, the following Official Basic Rules will serve for most everyday decisions and amateur-level play.

OFFICIAL RULES OF RPS—BASIC EDITION

The Prime

The prime is the ritual used to get players in synch with each other so they can deliver their throws simultaneously. It is the action of retracting one's fist from full-arm extension toward the shoulder and then back to full extension. This phase is critically important. If at any time the players are not in synch with their primes, then play must stop and begin again. Having players deliver their throws at the same time is critical to ensuring a fair match. Priming conventions generally fall into two classes:

1. **European Prime:** Three-prime shoot. Players pump their arms in unison three times before starting the approach phase.

2. **North American Prime:** Two-prime shoot. Players pump their arms in unison twice before starting the approach phase.

As an objection to using RPS, critics often cite different priming conventions. But RPS is no different than other international sports: European hockey is played on a larger ice surface than North American hockey. Canadian and American football is played with three and four downs respectively.

Suckering the Prime

It cannot be said often enough how important it is to establish the number of primes to be used before play commences, especially for the player who is accustomed to abiding by the two-prime shoot. If an opponent recognizes a player as a two-primer, he may try to initiate play without confirming the number of primes. The obvious reason being that he hopes to sucker the other player

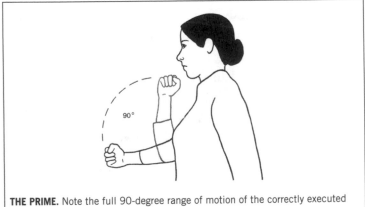

THE PRIME. Note the full 90-degree range of motion of the correctly executed prime as demonstrated above.

into revealing the first throw, then claim to have thought it was a three-prime format. Be forewarned that your opponent may "kindly" offer to replay the game, but he has now gained insight into your first-throw instincts without revealing his own, and thus he will be able to use this knowledge in the rematch. The official rule in this instance is that the players did not deliver simultaneously and therefore a rethrow is required.

SPOTTING THE BEGINNER

When you suspect an opponent is inexperienced or a beginner, a devious ploy to determine if this is indeed the case is to inquire whether he would rather play by International or European priming conventions. Should your opponent explain that although he is proficiently schooled in both styles, he has recently returned from abroad and would much prefer to play by the European conventions, your suspicions are confirmed. Your opponent is simply blustering; the only right answer would be that it hardly matters since these priming conventions are identical.

The Approach

The approach is the transition phase between the final prime and the delivery. As one's arm makes its final descent, a player is required to make a decision about the throw he will make. The approach begins at the shoulder following the final prime and ends when the arm makes a 90-degree angle with the player's body. Players must re-

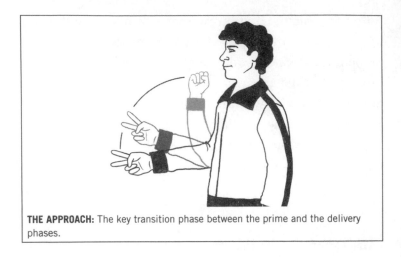

THE APPROACH: The key transition phase between the prime and the delivery phases.

veal their chosen throw to their opponent prior to reaching the 90-degree mark. Any throw delivered past this critical point must be considered a Forced Rock (since this is the position the hand would have been in upon crossing the 90-degree mark).

Players should make a reasonable effort to maintain the priming position during the approach phase. Many players see it as "the no-man's-land" and may attempt to make final adjustments that can result in critical blunders in their delivery. For example, some players will use a technique called shadowing to attempt to subtly move their fingers in an attempt to mislead a hand-watching opponent. This activity is not technically illegal unless the hand makes a decisive throw and then switches to another at the point of delivery.

The Delivery

Once firmly in the approach phase, it is time to shift focus to the delivery. Since the hand is technically already in the Rock position, it must either be switched to another throw or remain as Rock. Deciding what to throw at this point is necessary. Release the throw too early, and you risk your opponent reading the throw and adjusting accordingly. Release too late, and you risk a foul or a Forced Rock.

Players must deliver their throws at precisely the same time. Many recreational players choose to use their other palm as a platform to deliver their throws. This allows them to bounce their throwing hand off this hand platform during the prime and slam the fist down upon delivery to ensure a timely delivery while creating a pleasant clapping sound. Most serious players find that the platform constricts their motion and brands them as rookies.

The Three Throws

Although there are no points for style in an RPS match, delivering throws with an eye for good form is something that all players need to keep in mind. Delivering that perfectly executed Rock will not only impress opponents and spectators but will make the player feel better about his own game. Each throw requires a different delivery technique, and each will be examined in detail.

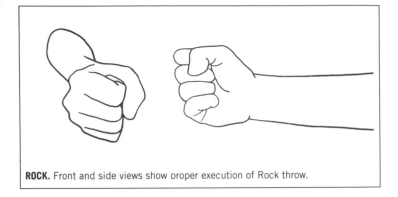

ROCK. Front and side views show proper execution of Rock throw.

Rock is represented by a closed fist with the thumb generally resting on the outside or top of the hand. The fist should be tight and decisive, with the knuckles of the fingers perpendicular to the ground and directed at the opponent. A little-known subtlety about Rock is that it is almost identical in every way to the priming position. Therefore players do not need to expend extra effort during the approach phase to achieve the optimum release for Rock.

Paper is represented by stretching all fingers forward and placing palm flat and parallel to the ground. The alternate palm-up form of Paper delivery, commonly referred to as "Feed the Pony," is also acceptable. This variation is grudgingly recognized in world-class competition because it incorporates the important 90-degree wrist turn that is shared with the palm-down approach. Which format to choose should be dictated by personal style and taste, but players should understand that the palm-down approach is considered technically better form.

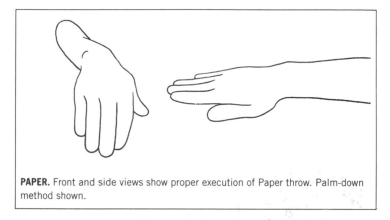

PAPER. Front and side views show proper execution of Paper throw. Palm-down method shown.

Team UK member Dougal Kerr *(left)* demonstrates the effectiveness of the "Feed the Pony" variation of Paper, which is considered acceptable due to the 90-degree wrist rotation. Referee is Elizabeth Bromstein. (Photo by Mark Coatsworth)

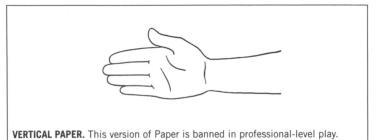

VERTICAL PAPER. This version of Paper is banned in professional-level play.

VERTICAL PAPER

Special mention must be made regarding the use of Vertical Paper, which has been banned in professional-level play due to its close resemblance to a handshake. Vertical Paper can easily be mistaken for the traditional sign of resignation, which is commonly offered by an outmatched opponent unwilling to continue a match. In addition, Vertical Paper, if delivered lazily, can often be mistaken for a poorly thrown Scissors.

Scissors is delivered with the fist perpendicular to ground with the index and middle finger—separated by no less than a 30-degree angle—extended firmly and decisively pointed toward the opponent. Players need note that Scissors is not delivered with a 90-degree turn of the wrist (i.e., Flat Scissors). The reason for this is obvious: in order for Scissors actually to cut Paper, the throw needs to be at a 90-degree angle to Paper. Further, if Scissors is delivered flat, it can be confused with Paper, should it be delivered in a sloppy fashion.

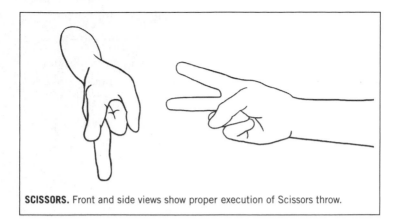

SCISSORS. Front and side views show proper execution of Scissors throw.

THE FORM CRITIC

Should you get bested in the first game of a two out of three, a good technique is to compliment your opponent on his selection of throws, then offer some suggestions on how he could improve his form. This will solidify your position as the more experienced player, despite having lost the first round. Having an opponent realize that you hold more knowledge is often enough to rattle him and force a mistake in the following rounds. Suggested banter includes:

"Nice Rock you threw. Your delivery was a little loose, though; tightening it up might take your game to an even higher level."

"That Paper delivery really brings attention to your nails. How long have you been biting them?"

"Nice win. I trust you understand that your sloppy Scissors delivery would earn you a warning from the ref, had we been in competitive play."

Assessment

Players should leave their throw positions visible until both players have had a chance to assess the outcome and determine a winner. Once a winner has been confirmed, by both parties or by a presiding official, players may remove their fists from the field of play and begin the next round or the match postanalysis.

PREGAME RITUAL

In order to be certain of a fair game, players should discuss the following three steps before every match. They are very simple and can be handled in a few seconds.

Step 1—Deciding on a Decision

Players must first establish what decision needs to be made. Generally this is easy because RPS is often suggested after a potential conflict arises. If it becomes impossible for players to agree on a potential decision, the game can be played for honor instead.

Step 2: Priming Convention

Players must agree on what priming convention is to be used. Where a player spent his childhood years is usually the determining influence on the prime. Most World RPS–sanctioned events adhere to the International Priming Standard Convention (IPSC), which uses the three-prime shoot. Either two or three primes are acceptable, as long as both players have agreed in advance. As a general rule and as a courtesy to the home player, the priming convention should default to the player who is considered on "local turf."

Local Turf

It can be difficult to determine "local turf" when both players are from out of town—for instance, when one RPS enthusiast meets another on vacation. This is where common sense and manners should be the guide. Should one vacationer have a friend or relative who is a local, then that person can lay claim to a "local linkage" and has the right to request the use of his regular priming convention. Should no one have a local linkage (a common situation at island resorts), then a query can be made of any passing local residents. They are usually more than happy to relay the standard local custom and may even wish to join in should they also be enthusiasts.

Note: Many enthusiasts often employ this technique simply as a way to meet local people while on holiday; in many cases these develop into lifelong friendships and/or valuable worldwide contacts.

Step 3: Round Determination

Players establish the number of wins required in order to reach a decision. The default choice is best of one, but a best two out of three is generally preferred because it opens up the strategic options considerably for the schooled player.

The Rounder's Ploy

Consider the following situation:

Mike: Hey, there's only one slice of pizza left.

Ian: Let's RPS for it.

Mike: Great idea. Ready? Okay, one, two, three, shoot!

(Mike throws Rock; Ian throws Paper.)

Ian: Sorry dude, I win. (begins to move hand toward final slice)

Mike: Hold on! We're playing best two out of three!

In the above example, Mike used a critical loophole to his advantage. Technically, these players never established how many games they were going to play in order to resolve the conflict. This is known as the rounder's ploy. Obviously, if Mike had won the first round, he would have claimed the coveted last slice for himself. Generally after such a ploy an argument will ensue between the winner and the loser, which, in addition to causing additional conflict, often results in a cold slice of pizza. Ian will tell Mike that he is cheating and that they were playing a one-round match. Mike will counter that it is a well-established fact that he *always* plays a best two of three, so he naturally assumed the same for this match. He may even offer his first-round Rock as evidence of this fact. "Well, had I known, I obviously would not have come out so strong with that Rock," Mike will say. Less experienced or meek players often fall prey to this ploy and capitulate. Although Mike will still be at a disadvantage, because he will have to win the next two games to get the slice, by employing this tactic he will turn his initial loss into a possible win.

Countering the Rounder's Ploy

Using the rounder's ploy is an underhanded tactic. Were these players not such good friends, it could have resulted in fisticuffs. For this reason, the rounder's ploy is frowned upon in RPS circles. After all, RPS is intended to resolve disputes, not create them. The counter for the rounder's ploy is to stand firm and quote section 1.2 of the World RPS Society's Official Rules and Regulations of the Grand Sport of Rock Paper Scissors: "If no agreement can be made, the match defaults to a single round format."

Note: Even if the player is unable to remember the specific rule number, it is often a good tactic to make up a number; players who quote rules numbers are very rarely challenged.

OUTCOMES

Within the RPS system, each of the noble throws is held in perfect balance against the others. The following table is a handy all-in-one reference guide to outcomes of potential matchups. While any player with enough time may think it's easier simply to memorize the table, players truly wishing to improve their game would be much better advised to gain a full understanding of the principles behind why each throw wins or loses. For instance, understanding that Scissors wins by actually cutting Paper will provide the player with a great visual reference that he can call upon should he become momentarily confused in the heat of battle.

THROW RESOLUTION

| | | PLAYER A THROWS | | |
		ROCK	PAPER	SCISSORS
PLAYER B THROWS	**ROCK**	Stalemate	Player A wins	Player B wins
	PAPER	Player B wins	Stalemate	Player A wins
	SCISSORS	Player A wins	Player B wins	Stalemate

HOW DOES ROCK BEAT SCISSORS?

It comes down to how a player views the game from a philosophical perspective. A player who prefers an offensive or aggressive style of RPS generally falls into the traditional Western approach and believes that Rock crushes Scissors. Proponents of the Eastern view, identifying with the conflict resolution nature of the game, take the pacifist approach that Scissors are dulled by Rock. In this way, Scissors are rendered less effective as a tool instead of being violently crushed.

How Does Scissors Beat Paper?

Although there is no quarrel about the fact that Scissors cuts Paper, fringe forces within the RPS community have often suggested that Scissors may not be able to cut Paper fully in a single stroke, and that more than one win would be required for Scissors to cut Paper. The official position of the World RPS Society is quite clear on the matter. In a landmark speech at the opening ceremonies of the 1963 Official Year of the Rock celebrations, Chairman Wojek Smallsoa delivered his opinion to the thunderous applause of society members: "It is assumed that Scissors are considered sharp enough, as well as long enough, to cut Paper in half with one firm snip. To even suggest the possibility that Paper may need to be cut twice is not only cowardly, but reprehensible."

How Does Paper Beat Rock?

As the game became more popular through the ages and players began seeking to understand the deeper concepts, questions such as "Just how does Paper beat Rock anyway?" became all too common. While those of an impatient and violent temperament find the notion of Paper winning against Rock to be counterintuitive, holders of this attitude miss the symbolic distinction. So suggestions that a really big Rock would tear or pin down a small piece of Paper are actually misguided. It does not matter what the relative proportions of the elements are; the issue is temporal in nature. Paper is representative of trees and, given sufficient time, tree roots will cover, penetrate, and even crush rocks.

STALEMATE

When players deliver identical throws, it is considered a stalemate. In the case of a stalemate, players simply rethrow until a win or loss situation results. Stalemates can often be confusing for beginner players, but they are great opportunities to take a short pause and reassess both opponent and strategy. Many professional-level players will intentionally attempt to force multiple stalemates in order to wear down opponents or expose clues regarding opponents' playing styles.

With an understanding of the basics of the game, the novice player is ready to go out and make some decisions. However, simply knowing the rules of the game will leave one unprepared when faced with a skilled opponent. The wise beginner will seek to grasp the fundamental strategy behind the game prior to active participation.

3

Basic Strategies

ROCK	PAPER	SCISSORS
POWER	STEALTH	INGENUITY

"To the beginner the choices are few;
to the expert the choices are many."

—From *The Trio of Hands* by Wojek Smallsoa,
chairman, World RPS Society Steering Committee

In order to appreciate the subtle and sometimes pro-found tactics associated with Rock Paper Scissors, one must first understand the fact that strategy does indeed play a role in the game. Acceptance of this fact differentiates the unranked novice from the player of a higher order.

Rock Paper Scissors is, at its core, about making a selection. Better players make better choices. Players collect, interpret, and ignore information both prior to and during the match. They must then make their choices. In turn, their opponents analyze these choices. The result is a tangled dance of strategy and counter-strategy, one that can be difficult for the casual player to appreciate. This chapter is designed to give the novice player insight into the basic strategic precepts, as well as ammunition against RPS detractors.

One often hears, spewing from the gaping maws and vacant minds of the ill informed, that Rock Paper Scissors is merely a game of random or unpredictable outcome. While an understandable position for the small-minded (often referred to in RPS circles as "Coin Tossers," a reference to the mid-nineteenth century that highlights the rivalry between RPS players and enthusiasts of lesser games), this is a fallacy. Human beings are utterly incapable of acting in a purely random fashion, despite appearances. Everything we do has some motivation behind it. This is certainly not to say that humans are always rational or logical, only that there is some kernel of a reason nestled somewhere in the dark caverns of the brain.

CHAOTIC VS. RANDOM

Chaos: Unpredictable and seemingly random behavior occurring in a system which should be governed by deterministic laws.

—*Oxford Concise Science Dictionary*

When considering the full range of an individual's behavior, it is difficult to predict what someone will do next. However, when we limit that behavior to those actions taken in the world of RPS, with its defined rules and three possible outcomes, making some educated guesses is possible. Even the layperson, once enlightened, can discern clues about an opponent's next play. So while RPS is not random, it is chaotic. This distinction is an important one: if a system is not truly random, then correct interpretation of information at hand can lead to a better chance of success.

The undulations of the stock market are considered chaotic because while they are governed by the easily understood principles of buying and selling; no one can tell with absolute certainty what will occur next. Despite the chaos, many traders have made successful careers interpreting the fluctuations accurately enough to generate significant profit. For the purposes of RPS, chaos means that if a player can correctly discern the exact state of his opponent's mind, as well as the process he uses to determine his next throw, then theoretically the player can correctly infer his opponent's next move. In contrast, random, from a mathematical perspective, means that an outcome happens without any predictability at all.

Contrary to popular belief, not even computers are capable of completely random behavior, either, since they operate according to a set of rules established by human beings. In 2003, the World RPS Society made a bold step by authorizing the entrance of a player guided by a computer program to compete at the World Championships. The computer program, called Deep Mauve, was used to supply the player with a series of throws in an attempt to better approximate randomness. As was predicted by many leading RPS mavens, the Deep Mauve team did not make it past the qualifying round. The failure of the computer has sent those few in the random-is-the-best-strategy camp scrambling to redefine their argument.

CHANCE IN RPS

Much to the dismay of RPS-playing parents, many elementary-school teachers have used Rock Paper Scissors to illustrate probability. Probability refers to the chance of a particular outcome occurring within a defined set of possible variables. So, for example, there are three possible outcomes that result in an odd number when rolling a six-sided die: one, three, and five. There are six possible outcomes overall. Therefore the probability of rolling an odd number is three in six, or 50 percent, as long as we are not in a crooked casino. However, in RPS, all of the players are crooked, so to speak. Each will make a conscious choice of which throw to make with the express desire of humiliating his adversary. So to assign basic probability to an RPS match would be a grave error, unless the player's aspiration reaches only to a height of mediocrity.

Take, for example, this hypothetical question from a sixth-grade math test:

Question: Jimmy and Janie are playing a game of Rock Paper Scissors. Each can play only one of the three throws. What is the probability that Jimmy will play Rock next?
Answer: 1 in 3.

The above question displays a deplorable lack of knowledge regarding RPS game play. This pitiful explanation does not contain remotely enough information to make an accurate prediction. Is Jimmy a good player? Has he played against Janie before? Are they playing with two or three primes? What did Jimmy play last? Is Janie right- or left-handed? Does Jimmy have a tattoo?

Janie and Jimmy play RPS. Janie correctly predicts Jimmy's ruinous play of Paper.

These are just a few of the factors that could drastically affect the outcome. Perhaps the question should more accurately include: "For the purposes of this asinine test, assume that Jimmy and Janie both suffer from a debilitating mental defect that renders them incapable of forming a coherent thought or retaining any memories." Ignorant questions such as the one listed above have no doubt robbed an entire generation of reaching their potential in the sport.

Aside from the demeaning notion that chance plays a role, RPS played by humans does not conform to the law of averages. Probability would dictate that over the long run roughly one-third of all of the throws ever made would be Rock, one-third Paper, and one-third Scissors. After careful observation of numerous championships, in which literally thousands of throws were made, the World RPS Society knows this not the case. This notion suggests a hidden agenda from educators claiming that RPS players have no intent in their throws.

Opening Moves

While the number of opening techniques is limited only by the imagination, the most common opening throws tend to result in Rock, Paper, or Scissors. Proper use of the opening move is crucial to success, and it can secure the advantage for the remainder of the match. Let us take each of the basic opening moves in turn:

Rock

Represented as it is by a closed fist, Rock is commonly perceived as the most aggressive throw. It taps into memories of fistfights, and it conjures up images of tall and unmoving mountains, rugged boulders, and the stone axe of the cavemen. Without realizing it, most players think of Rock as a weapon and will fall back on it for protection when other strategies appear to be failing.

On the other hand, use of Rock when on the offensive is a sign of overconfidence and an obvious attempt to intimidate an opponent. Among beginners in the sport, Rock is by far the most common opening throw. Rock is a powerful move that must be handled with finesse in order to avoid overextending oneself.

Rock also happens to be the most effortless of throws, and fast reactions are never required to employ it with success. By careful examination of the options and atmosphere of play, a well-placed Rock will render useless a carelessly thrown Scissors every time.

ROCK (A): Typical Rock player, prethrow

ROCK (B): Typical Rock player in action

Rock is	Player's mind-set
Overbearing	I am confident, perhaps even arrogant.
Aggressive	I am seeking the quick win.
Powerful	I am stronger than you.
Blunt	I act before thinking.

Paper

Paper is often considered the subtlest of the three throws. There is nothing aggressive about the limp documents that move across our desks and through our offices. Even the gesture used to represent Paper is peaceful—an open palm much like the gesture used in a salute or a handshake. Historically, an open palm has been a sign of friendship and peace because an open hand cannot hold a weapon. Some players, who subconsciously perceive Paper as a sign of weakness or surrender, will shy away from using it entirely or will drop it from their game when they are falling behind.

On the other hand, Paper also connects with a player's perceptions about writing. There is quiet power in the printed word. It contains the ability to lay off thousands of employees, declare war against nations, spread scandal, or confess love. Paper, in short, has power over masses. The fate of the entire world is determined by print. As such, some players perceive Paper as a subtle attack, the victory of modern culture over barbarism. Such players may use Paper to assert their superiority and dignity.

Paper is the most challenging of the basic opening moves because it requires the manual displacement of all five digits in addition to a full 90-degree wrist rotation. It is, therefore, generally viewed as the least obvious of opening throws. Should a player open with Paper, rest assured that a counter of Scissors will cut it down to size.

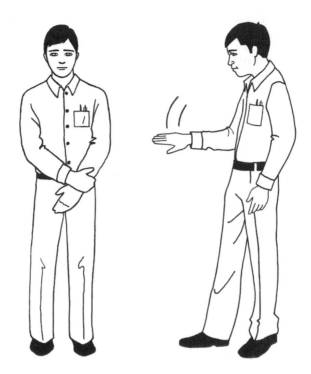

PAPER (A): Typical Paper player, prethrow

PAPER (B): Typical Paper player in action

Paper is	Player's mind-set
Protective	I feel threatened.
Passive	I conserve my strength.
Thoughtful	I am open-minded.
Flimsy	I am easily influenced.

Scissors

Scissors are a tool. As children, we use them to cut construction paper for craft projects. As adults, we may cut cloth for clothing or use scissors to open irritating plastic packaging. Scissors are associated with industry, craftwork, and construction. There is still a certain amount of aggression associated with scissors; they are, after all, sharp and dangerous implements. Different from the thuglike force of Rock, Scissors represent aggression that is controlled, contained, and rechanneled into something constructive.

In RPS, Scissors is often perceived as a clever or crafty throw, a well-planned outflanking maneuver. As such, players are more likely to use Scissors when they are confident or winning. Opening with Scissors presumes that an opponent has tight control over their aggressive tendencies and therefore will not open with Rock. One of the main pitfalls of opening with Scissors is the tendency of many to reveal the throw too early, allowing an experienced opponent to easily counter.

SCISSOR (A): Typical Scissor player, prethrow

SCISSOR (B): Typical Scissor player in action

Scissors is	Player's mind-set
Devious	I am not to be trusted.
Ingenious	I am calculating.
Reactive	I may switch tactics quickly.
Sharp	I will surprise you.

Psyching Out the Psychic

True psychics are rarely encountered, but in case you find yourself playing against someone with second sight, we recommend that you practice your throws while thinking of the name of another throw. Instead of thinking of a throw by its rightful name, think of it by the name of the throw that beats it. Thus, when throwing Scissors, think Rock. When throwing Rock, think Paper. When throwing Paper, think Scissors. This results in the psychic discerning your intention to play a certain throw, then reacting and offering the throw that beats it, all the while you are actually using the throw that beats your opponent's. Practice it enough, and it will become second nature. One caveat, this effect may become permanent and muddle your playing style for tournaments.

Gambits

"Gambit: a series of three successive moves made with strategic intention."

—*The Master's Guide to Rock Paper Scissors*

To demonstrate how knowing one's opponent can affect play, imagine playing RPS against an opponent who has just thrown two Rocks in a row. Naturally, one should question whether this player has the courage to play Rock for a third time and complete the Avalanche gambit. If this information affects the next throw, then the player has just begun to grasp the most basic strategy of RPS, the use of gambits.

The use of gambits in competitive RPS has been one of the greatest and most enduring breakthroughs in RPS strategy. "Strategic intent" means that the three throws are selected beforehand as part of a planned sequence. Selecting throws in advance helps prevent unconscious patterns from forming and can sometimes reduce the subtle signals that give away the next throw, often called "tells." Choosing throws in groups of three can help to prevent a player from switching to a purely reactive game while leaving numerous decision points to keep the strategy adaptable. Gambits are the focal point of beginner strategy and form the basis of many advanced strategies.

Most games of RPS are played as best-of-three matches; therefore, counting throws by threes is logical, since the correct choice of a three-throw sequence will usually take care of an unsuspecting opponent, even allowing for a single loss or stalemate.

To veteran players, gambits are also frequently used as a shorthand way to discuss matches without resorting to a long list of throws. For example, one player might be overheard saying to another "Excellent match, Charles. Your inspired use of a Crescendo in the opening set negated the early lead of my Toolbox."

THE GREAT EIGHT GAMBITS

The mathematically inclined will quickly realize that there are only twenty-seven possible gambits. All of them have been used and documented in tournament play. Each has several names, depending on the geographical region of the players. There is no such thing as a "new" gambit.

The Great Eight Gambits are the eight deemed to be the most historically significant and the most widely employed. They also happen to be the only eight gambits in which there is near unanimous consent on the names. There is nothing about these eight that make them superior to any other gambits, although as a group they can be very effective. Several high-level players have built careers on just these eight gambits. They are, sorted alphabetically by their most common names, the following:

AVALANCHE

ROCK ROCK ROCK

A subtle, yet aggressive gambit. It was the first of the triple gambits developed in the early 1890s. The Avalanche is a relentless and devastating offensive maneuver; executing it requires bravado bordering on recklessness.

THE BUREAUCRAT

PAPER   PAPER   PAPER

Formerly known as Confetti, the deadpan delivery of three successive Papers is the ultimate in passive-aggressive play. Team Bureaucrat, who have gone on record as stating that "Paper is the new Rock," had at least one representative in the final sixteen at the 2003 World Championships.

THE CRESCENDO

PAPER   SCISSORS   ROCK

The slow-building nature of this gambit makes it a very elegant opening series. The devastating Rock is the coup de grâce that gives the gambit its name.

DENOUEMENT

ROCK   SCISSORS   PAPER

The Denouement is the mirror of the Crescendo and uses a cooling-down approach. When used in tandem with the Crescendo, the result is often a baffled opponent.

FISTFUL O'DOLLARS

ROCK   PAPER   PAPER

This move took the 1967 RPS World Championships by surprise and is arguably still one of the great surprise offensive moves. The rapid switch from offensive to defensive play can force an opponent into a vulnerable spot.

PAPER DOLLS

The complexity of this series is belied by its apparent simplicity. Paper levels the playing field and is followed by a couple of quick and sneaky Scissors, which makes it an extremely effective gambit against the unwary.

SCISSOR SANDWICH

An invasive and devious gambit. While not the most offensive of the gambits, its main purpose is to unsettle the opponent through the use of the concealed Scissors.

TOOLBOX

Effective use of the Toolbox requires steady hands and steely nerves. Given the puerile popularity of Rock, this gambit is not suggested for use against beginners.

MIRROR PLAY

When RPS players are evenly matched or delivering similar strategies, the result can often be an embarrassing string of ties or stalemates, referred to as Mirror Play. Whereas a stalemate is a single tie and cause for a rethrow, Mirror Play is a series of stalemates. It is often the result of two players attempting similar strategies. Mirroring one's opponent in a sequence of five or six identical throws can be disconcerting and never fails to increase the level of tension surrounding a match. Depending upon how an opponent handles stress, intentionally mirroring can wear down his reserves and leave him easy prey to a surprise attack.

Mirror Play (for example, a situation in which both players throw Scissors over and over again) needs to be treated as a special situation. For example, two opponents have each delivered three successive Rocks in a row. Both players are now involved in a game of chicken. Each is wondering how long to hold out. When will the opponent's resolve break to play Paper for the win? Should a player risk Scissors, hoping that the opponent is about to crack?

While Mirror Play can be highly stressful, it is also a crowd pleaser. During the 2003 World Championship semifinal match between Marc Rigaux and Patrick Merry, head referee Brent Andruko felt it necessary to call a

Head Referee Brent Andruko (center) calls for a brief time out for Silver Medalist Marc Rigaux (left) and Bronze Medalist Patrick Merry (right) to halt a Mirror Play. (Photo by Mark Coatsworth)

time-out during the fourth set after the players had fallen into an extended Mirror Play, to the delight of the audience members, who had worked themselves into a lather.

As a defensive ploy, one can retreat into a Mirror Play scenario in order to recover from a loss. If taken in stride, a short series of Mirror Plays can be a welcome respite during a hectic match, allowing a player valuable time to reconsider strategy. One must also commit to memory the counterstrategy when a Mirror Play is an opponent's intention; it might just be the opportunity to pounce.

Wits and Dexterity

It is common among dullards to avoid playing RPS and retreat to less-complicated decision-making games, such as One Potato, Two Potato; Engine, Engine, Number Nine; or Odds and Evens. This is due to the mental challenges associated with RPS. However, it is important to note that physical prowess also plays an important role in this sport. The manual dexterity of delivering multiple throws in quick succession can be taxing for some, but it is the small-motor skills, finer muscular movements, and psychology associated with the game that separates it from all others. Shrewd players must quickly progress to using ever more cunning RPS strategies and tactics.

4

ADVANCED STRATEGIES

"What the hell were you thinking out there, kid?
I told you never to use your Rock when
backed into a corner."

James "Wooly" Hupdoorf, leading RPS coach,
to Chester Winkerton, after his devastating loss
at the 1945 World Championships

When important decisions are on the line, one cannot simply rely upon basic strategy to win. One must break out the advanced strategies of RPS to stay one step ahead of the opponent. While there are enough strategies in use around the world to fill a thousand books, we shall focus on several of the most common defensive and offensive strategies.

Defensive Strategies

Spring Loading
Difficulty: *

Keeping a pair of spring-loaded Scissors handy is a must for any serious player. Spring loading involves applying pressure against the thumb with the index and middle (or "Scissor fingers") during the approach. This allows for a quicker release of Scissors, thus catching the opponent completely off guard. Holding Scissors under camouflage until the last possible moment has many defensive benefits; however, excessive use of spring loading will result in a visible tell (see Smoothing Your Tells below) that can make Scissors easy prey for the watchful player's Rock.

Known counterstrategies: Rock

The Urbanus Defense
Difficulty: *

Well-known U.S. player C. Urbanus popularized this strategy, employing it with limited success at the World Championship level. This strategy is the intentional loss of the first throw in a best-of-three game. The purpose of sacrificing the first throw is twofold. First, the loss instills a false sense of confidence in the opponent; second, it forces the opponent (via the opening throw) to reveal valuable clues about his overall line of attack. While easy to accomplish, heavy reliance on the Urbanus Defense without any other strategies has proven highly ineffective.

Known counterstrategies: Ineptitude

Cloaking
Difficulty: **

The ability to conceal or "cloak" a throw of Paper is one of the first skills that an aspiring RPS competitor must master. The art of cloaking is to hold the approach until the final split-second prior to delivery. The key to this strategy rests upon the remarkable similarity between the priming position and Rock position. Effectively cloaking disguises a Paper as a Rock for a time. One must be exceptionally careful to accomplish the switch to Paper before the angle between forearm and upper arm reaches 90 degrees. This is a tricky maneuver and requires expert timing. A cloak pulled too late is at best a Rock and at worst (under the sharp eyes of a referee) a disqualification.

Known counterstrategies: Spring-loaded Scissors

Pattern Shattering
Difficulty: ****

Humans are unable to make their throws truly random. The advanced player will take advantage of this fact and attempt to identify and avoid his own natural patterns of throws. One common pattern is known as Escher's Staircase, in which one plays the throw that beats the throw he delivered previously, i.e., Rock followed by Paper, followed by Scissors, followed by Rock, and so on). Another is the tendency for beginners to repeat a throw when faced with a stalemate. Discover personal patterns and keep a list of gambits handy to shake things up when faced with the nagging suspicion that you are becoming predictable.

Known counterstrategies: Hypnosis, distraction

Throw Counting
Difficulty: *****

Throw counting is the act of keeping mental records during the game of all the opponent's throws in order to spot short-term patterns. The key here is accuracy under pressure. It can be difficult to keep one's mind on the game while simultaneously making mental notes, which is why this strategy does not fall into the basic category.

Known counterstrategies: Constant chattering and shouting out random throws and numbers will usually muddle up the throw counter.

Chaos Play
Difficulty: ∞

An opponent cannot predict a player's next action if the player does not know it himself. For many, "chasing chaos" is the pinnacle of defensive play. Many prominent players—such as 2002 World Champion Peter Lovering—admit to clearing their mind before the throw and seeking enlightenment through Zen or other philosophies and theologies. Some claim to achieve a chaotic state through meditation, channeling, or other spiritual methods. Others simply trust their emotions. In the most extreme cases, chaos players experiment with mind-altering drugs. From a technical standpoint, chaos play usually involves determining throws based upon a series of simple rules that combine and become progressively more complex with each throw.

Pete Lovering hoists the World RPS Cup high after becoming the 2002 World RPS Champion. (Photo by Kathy Maukner)

Known counterstrategies: The only known strategy effective against chaos play is to respond with chaos play; unfortunately, this is successful only 50 percent of the time.

SMOOTHING YOUR TELLS

Tells, the unconscious signals a player reveals, come in many forms; for example, facial expressions, eye movements, muscle tension, stance, galvanic skin response, and other forms of body language. Learning to recognize the signals that give a player away to his opponent requires a keen eye and self-awareness and is usually best done in front of a mirror. (Some people feel so foolish playing RPS in front of a mirror that they will adopt completely different tells than those they typically exhibit in tournament play. In those cases, watching videotaped matches of yourself is often a good method of discovering one's own tells.)

Once aware of tells, a player should work at minimizing their visibility. Adopting a comfortable stance should be the first goal; when the body is relaxed there is less overall muscle tension and therefore fewer muscular tells. Facial and eye expressions are more difficult to eliminate. Listed below are several of the more common tells and how to smooth them.

NAME OF TELL	DESCRIPTION	HOW TO MINIMIZE
Rock Jaw	Players may exhibit tension around jaw muscles prior to throwing a Rock.	Breathing evenly through your nose can help to relax tense jaw muscles.
Scissor Fingers	Excess tension between index finger and thumb causes a small muscle to pop out in the hand, which indicates an imminent throw of Scissors. Technically this appears to be caused by excessive flexing of the intrinsic thenar group of muscles in the hand.	Keep hand relaxed and avoid excessive spring loading.
The Paper Hook	Some players display a tendency to curve their hand motion during approach toward the body immediately prior to throwing Paper. The motion follows a backward C-shape when viewed by the opponent (assuming right hand is used).	Practice throwing Paper very slowly while maintaining vertical motion of the prime. During competitions, avoid rushing your Paper throws.
The Switch-Up Shuffle	Many amateur players adjust their stance and shift their weight only when they transition from one throw to another, and maintain their stance when repeating throws.	Wear comfortable shoes when playing to minimize unconscious shuffling.

NAME OF TELL	DESCRIPTION	HOW TO MINIMIZE
Swaying	Some players show slight to severe swaying back and forth before initiating the prime, particularly when losing. This tell indicates a lack of confidence and a likely shift in strategies.	Keep feet shoulder width apart to maintain balance, and avoid excessive amounts of alcohol.

OFFENSIVE STRATEGIES

Exclusion Play
*Difficulty: **

Exclusion play involves limiting throws to only one or two options, thus avoiding one or more of the three throws. While choosing from one or two throws is far less taxing on the brain, effective exclusion play can be a grueling exercise in perseverance.

Known counterstrategies: Early recognition of exclusion play

The Viper
*Difficulty: ***

To use the viper is to lull the opponent into a weak position and then launch an attack at his most vulnerable moment. Use of repeated stalemates will force an opponent to reconsider his line of attack. It is precisely when an opponent is reevaluating his approach that he is defenseless against a surprise assault. Patience is vital. To accomplish a successful viper, one must be very familiar with the opponent's patterns and wait for the opportunity to arise. During the height of Team Bureaucrat's fame in the early 1920s, Michael "Cheeky" Bardley relied heavily upon this strategy and became legendary for maintaining his serenity for long periods of time, then he would strike while his opponent briefly let his defenses down.

Known counterstrategies: The mongoose defense. Stated simply, the mongoose is surprising an opponent before he has a chance to implement the viper strategy.

Broadcasting False Tells
Difficulty: ***

The essence of this strategy is the purposeful projecting of false muscle, stance, and eye cues to misdirect an opponent. This strategy should be used only against expert players, since it is ineffectual against players who are not sophisticated enough to watch for tells. Make sure not to wear gloves or sunglasses; otherwise, the effect is greatly reduced.

Known counterstrategies: Zoning out an opponent

Playing Switch

Difficulty: ***

Notorious U.S. player Master Roshambollah sent shock waves through the audience during the 2003 World Championships quarter finals when in a surprise offensive maneuver, he switched to his left hand mid-match. Switching hands can also be used as a defensive strategy to ward off hand fatigue in longer matches and tournaments. However, to be as effective with a non-dominant hand requires twice the commitment during training.

Known counterstrategies: Nerves of steel

PLAYING SWITCH. A normally right-handed player demonstrates a Paper delivery with a switch, or left-handed delivery.

Shadowing

Difficulty: *****

Shadowing is similar to cloaking, and also related to broadcasting false tells. It involves indicating one throw prior to throwing another at the last possible moment. This is extremely difficult and requires great care in execution. Referees generally take a dim view of shadowing, and, should there be any ambiguity about the throw, a player is likely to lose the point. There are two primary ways in which shadowing can be used. The first involves twitching fingers slightly during the prime. A hand-watching opponent may believe this to foreshadow a throw of Scissors or Paper. A more advanced method of shadowing is to change hand positions subtly multiple

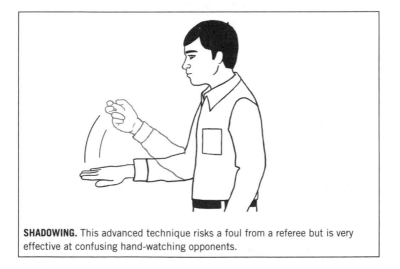

SHADOWING. This advanced technique risks a foul from a referee but is very effective at confusing hand-watching opponents.

times during the last prime. This has the potential to confuse or distract most opponents and will likely befuddle a hand watcher completely.

Known counterstrategies: Complaining to the ref and instant video replays

The Urbanus Offense
*Difficulty: *****

While much more difficult to accomplish, the Urbanus Offense is the flipside of the Urbanus Defense. Successful deployment involves intentionally winning the first round to put an opponent on the defensive. Of the two Urbanus strategies, the offensive maneuver can be used in isolation without diluting its efficacy.

Known counterstrategies: None

Paper Clipping
*Difficulty: *****

Paper clipping is a broad term referring to persuading (or suckering) an opponent into a throw of Paper. The clipping comes in the form of the response of Scissors. While exceedingly difficult to accomplish effectively, it is the closest thing in RPS to an unbeatable offensive strategy.

Known counterstrategies: None

• • •

While not all of the strategies will be effective in the blundering hands of the neophyte, familiarity with them is crucial for playing above the level of the recreational player.

5

BUILDING YOUR STRATEGY

"No two games are the same."

Custardchuk,
Australian RPS Player of the Year, 1984

All the theory in the world will not help a player un-less he can put strategy into practice. This section examines how to use inner strength to develop a unique playing style. For example, some players are natural "scripters" and plan throws weeks before a high-level tournament, whereas other players rely on quick reflexes or logical reasoning to spot an opponent's sloppy moves. This section will reference material from the basic and advanced strategies chapters. The end of this chapter also features the famous Martok-Singleton personality test, which will provide the key to unlocking hidden RPS strengths.

Knowing the Opponent

Greater even than stone, manuscript, or tempered steel, the most potent weapon of **RPS** is psychology. When faced with a new opponent, the superior **RPS** player will seek to categorize his adversary into one or more of the basic character types.

The Rank Novice

This sort is fairly easy to classify by a characteristically cavalier attitude and lack of knowledge regarding the game's subtleties. Casually asking, "Did you perhaps read the article in *Think Three Magazine* on the Rock Two Three Switch strategy?," is usually sufficient to elicit the novice's trademark blank stare of ignorance. The attire and deportment displayed is frequently inappropriate for whatever venue the novice blunders into. The rank novice will usually open with Rock and, due to its simplicity, rely upon it heavily throughout the match.

The Paper Tiger

The Paper Tiger is a half step above the novice. This type is recognized by a brash attitude, combined with a preference for distracting clothing and intoxicating substances. At tournaments they can usually be found in outlandish costumes whoring themselves for the media. For example, the hideously named Team Slut is a World Championship–level team composed entirely of Paper Tigers and has yet to field a single player past the qualifying round. While Paper Tigers are likely to have some limited familiarity with RPS jargon, do not be fooled. It is unlikely that they have studied strategy in any depth. They are also very likely to regale any unfortunate bystanders with outlandish tales of their RPS prowess and former tournament glory. These braggarts regard Paper as a sure-fire opener, and their flighty attitude will likely keep them from repeating a throw more than twice.

The Statistician

This is the most prevalent of the many forms of "scripters." Scripters preplan all of their moves sometimes weeks before a big match to work the kinks out of a strategy. What sets apart the Statistician from other scripters is an inexplicable impulse to play based upon probabilities. The Statistician is highly strung and may have some odd rituals prior to beginning play such as lining up personal items in a specific order, twitching, washing hands frequently, or murmuring audibly. A pad of paper, calculator, or personal digital assistant to take notes on play almost always accompanies the Statistician. They are easily rattled, so make sure to throw a few loose Scissors into the game to keep them on edge. Despite a commanding knowledge of RPS and its strategies, players of this ilk suffer from a constant focus on the next match at the expense of the current match. This is frequently their undoing in competitive play.

The Shamrock

Another highly ritualized player, but instead of the obsessive-compulsive behaviors of the Statistician, the Shamrock engages in a frequently irritating series of "good-luck" routines prior to play. These rituals may involve spitting into hands, constantly wearing the same clothing, praying, cracking knuckles, or avoiding stepping on any lines on the floor. Shamrocks will frequently mark themselves by referring to their playing career in terms of winning or losing streaks. They can be highly frustrating to play against, but their pathetic reliance upon luck usually makes them extremely predictable. Just about any coherent strategy will best the Shamrock; as a result, they are much more likely to infest dingy pubs in a quest for money matches than darken the registration tables of the more respectable tournaments.

Diamond in the Rough

This category comprises the unknown and undiscovered raw talent. Therefore, they are the most difficult of all players to spot. They are usually found at their first local tournament wandering aimlessly and absorbing the atmosphere before their first match. The best clue to finding these characters is to watch for an unusual amount of spectators and video cameras surrounding them at an otherwise insignificant match. Trainers and talent scouts are very quick to sniff out these players and can frequently be found hovering around a Diamond in the Rough player, leading to the popular RPS maxim, "See the scout and spot the threat." These players are often amazed at their own proficiency at the game and display very few outward clues of their inner gifts. While they may be unaware of the finer points of the game, they will display an uncanny genius for reactionary play. Players with this unspoiled talent combined with the right training and guidance usually evolve into the Professionals.

The best way to counter Diamonds in the Rough is to discover their weakest throw and focus efforts there. Without solid training they will likely heavily favor a single throw. Alternately, their ignorance of traditional RPS strategy can leave them vulnerable to many of the well-known gambits.

Devil May Care

A friendly charm, conversational demeanor, and equanimity while competing characterize Devil May Cares. This is a highly refined playing style, so do not be lulled into a false sense of security by their apparent don't-give-a-damnsmanship. Refining these traits can require years of study and competition experience. On the surface, they will feign a limited knowledge of the game and thus attempt to mimic the Rank Novice, but closer inspection should reveal highly developed finger muscles and a willingness to escalate the stakes at every opportunity. They may even lose the opening throw in a match (see Urbanus Defense) to lure a gullible fly into their web of strategy.

The Professional

In contrast to the Devil May Cares, the Professionals make no attempt to hide their skills. Their dress tends toward the formal. They usually have enough experience to size up an opponent's next move correctly and rarely is a mistake made. Any follower of the game should be familiar with several names of players in this category. Take every chance to engage players of this type, not because there is any hope of winning, but simply for the incredible learning opportunity presented by getting pulverized by a top player. By the time the World Championships whittle down to the top eight or sixteen, usually only the Professionals are left. Members of Team All to Flat based in New York have used a secret education facility since the 1950s to churn out dozens of high-caliber Professionals.

This is only a small sample of the various character

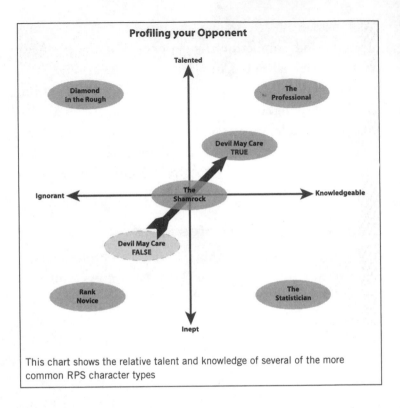

Profiling your Opponent

Talented

Diamond in the Rough

The Professional

Devil May Care TRUE

Ignorant ← The Shamrock → Knowledgeable

Devil May Care FALSE

Rank Novice

The Statistician

Inept

This chart shows the relative talent and knowledge of several of the more common RPS character types

types that can be seen on the tournament circuit. While there are many players who fit snugly into categories, some straddle one or more categories, and a select few completely defy all attempts at description.

Professional U.S. Player Benjamin Stein of Team All Too Flat in tournament action. (Photo courtesy of Team All Too Flat)

THE IMPORTANCE OF THE FIRST THROW

The first throw is a window into the style, strategy, and capabilities of an opponent. Specifically it is the first tangible evidence about what an opponent is thinking and how they have assessed an adversary's playing abilities. By this point one should be familiar with recognizing strategies, forming gambits, and categorizing an opponent. So it is the first throw that gives the chance to test pregame hypotheses. In fact, the wide-awake player will view the first throw merely as a confirmation of his beliefs.

Many players will lead with their strongest and most comfortable throw, so expect to see it pop up frequently during the game. The first throw is often the very same throw that an amateur opponent will rely upon when backed into a corner. An opening throw is also an opportunity to gauge an opponent's technical abilities on a physical level. An advanced player must be able to establish quickly whether the opponent has any obvious tells or whether he has mastered cloaking and shadowing techniques. Muscles at this point are as fresh as they will get during the match, so any tells spotted now should get only more pronounced as the game progresses and energy reserves begin to dwindle.

The results of the first throw are far-reaching. A quick win can establish dominance over an opponent and fracture his composure, whereas losing to an opponent can make him overconfident. However, often the best move for experienced players is to force a stalemate. A draw always favors the more experienced player by revealing the foibles of the feeble mind.

At one set apiece, you and your opponent face off to commence the final set. Your opponent is male, approximately thirty years old, with a beard, dressed in a fashionable outfit with a fairly pronounced receding hairline. In the last set he threw PRP to beat your RRR. What is your opening move?

A. Rock
B. Paper
C. Scissors

Answer: B—Paper. While all of the information should be considered, the giveaway here is the receding hairline. Many people suffering from hair loss are also xyrophobic, or have a fear of razors and other sharp cutting instruments. In RPS players this paralyzing condition leads to Scissors exclusionary strategies. The hypothesis is confirmed by his avoidance of Scissors in the second set, not to mention the beard. So if you know that your opponent is afraid of wielding Scissors, then Paper has a 50 percent chance of winning and a 50 percent chance of tying, thus making it the only logical choice.

SICILIAN REASONING

Sicilian reasoning is the cornerstone of developing unique strategies during a game situation. Sicilian reasoning cannot be preplanned; it is highly dependent upon the situation. It is an iterative process that builds upon itself and rapidly grows in complexity. The term was popularized in the movie *The Princess Bride,* in which the character Vizzini (a Sicilian) engages in a battle of wits to the death. His opponent, Westley, has poisoned one of two wine goblets, and Vizzini attempts to reason out which cup has the poison through a series of "if you know, that I know, that you know . . ." type statements.

The reasoning commences with an assumption and then layers questions regarding the opponent's awareness and possible reactions to this knowledge. See the chart below for the first three stages of reasoning.

	OFFENSIVE REASONING	DEFENSIVE REASONING
First Stage	What will my opponent do next?	What does my opponent believe I will do next?
Second Stage	How will my opponent react to what he thinks I will do next?	How does my opponent expect me to react to what I think he knows about my next move?
Third Stage	If my opponent is conscious that I know that he can discern what my next move will be, what will he throw next?	I am aware that my opponent knows that I have figured out that he knows what my next move will be, but if he knows that I am conscious of this, how will he react?

The trick with Sicilian reasoning is to know when to stop and when to continue layering questions on the original assumption. A fifth-stage defensive argument may be a work of logical genius, but in the process a player risks vastly overestimating his opponent's intellect.

RPS PERSONALITY TEST

The Martok-Singleton Player Type Test is the most reliable of the RPS profiling methods. Singlis Martok, of the World RPS Society Theoretical Throws Bureau, developed this test. Why the name Singleton appears after Martok remains a mystery, but the leading theory is that it is simply a bastardization of the author's first name and was included to make the test sound more credible.

This test is designed to assist a player in realizing which strategies are best by categorizing them into one of the Martok-Singleton player types.

Note: Be warned that if you choose to mark your answers within this book, you should not lend the book to anyone else or you will be disclosing very valuable information.

SECTION 1: Choose the answer that best reflects your attitudes and opinions. If neither represents you accurately, choose the least repugnant answer.

1. What is more fun for you:
a. Yelling at a subordinate
b. Interpreting Swedish furniture assembly instructions

2. Do you tend to notice:
a. A flaw in someone's aura
b. Loud and frightening noises

3. What is more appealing:
a. Filing a friend's taxes
b. Getting persecuted for your beliefs

4. Left to your own devices do you:
a. Panic
b. Pick a fight with whoever is handy

5. Do you view yourself as:
a. Easily manipulated
b. An expert in science fiction

6. What do you value more in others:
a. Subservience
b. Blind acceptance of a shared misconception

SECTION 2: This section includes some everyday situations in which you may find yourself. Choose the answer that best represents the action you would take for each situation. Be honest.

7. A friend has mistakenly e-mailed you a spreadsheet of his household expenses. What do you do?
a. Ignore the numbers in favor of searching for errors in his formulae.
b. Respond immediately and chastise him for overspending on auto insurance.
c. Tell your friend you want $1,000 or you will forward the information to a group of telemarketers.
d. Refuse to open it; but file it away in case you need it later.

8. You wake up to find yourself naked in the middle of an unknown forest. What is your first move?

a. Dig a pit trap with a series of sharp sticks at the bottom, cover the pit over with leaves, and then hide behind a tree while waiting for help to arrive.

b. Use this as an opportunity to begin a new life free from all material concerns.

c. Scream while proactively running around in circles until you succumb to exhaustion and ultimately die from exposure.

d. Wait for nightfall and walk toward the bright lights.

9. You have been passed over for a promotion at the cheese factory for the second year in a row. How do you react?

a. Spend another night by the TV crying over a wheel of brie.

b. Find out if your boss can stay afloat in the curd tank.

c. Remove the "Honk if you love Cheeses" promotional bumper sticker from the company delivery truck.

d. Arrange a delightful cheese plate and have it couriered to congratulate the new executive supervisor of veined cheeses.

10. You have been asked to make a speech at the grand opening of the Institute for Advanced Bureaucracy. The civil servants in attendance appear annoyed as you begin your discourse on "Downsizing the Government." What is your next move?

a. Trust that your passionate appeal will convert the unwashed heathens.

b. Cut the ribbon quickly and slip away before the networking event in the hospitality suite.

c. At the first sign of disapproval, switch topics to "Too Many Hands Make for Light Work."

d. Single out a few unattractive members of the audience for public ridicule.

11. While visiting your best friend, you are told that he recently caught his young son smoking; to punish him, he has locked the boy in a closet with three big cigars to finish. What do you do?

a. Discover whether the cigars were Cuban and then inquire politely whether there are any more about the house.

b. Marvel at the leniency of today's spineless parents.

c. Worry about the potential of a fire in the closet.

d. Reflect on how you wish your parents had allowed you to smoke in the house.

SCORING CHART: Circle each of your answers for each question and then total the number of answers from each column.

QUESTION	A	S	L	R
1	a		b	
2		a		b
3		b	a	
4	b			a
5			b	a
6	a	b		
7	c	d	a	b
8	a	b	d	c
9	b	d	c	a
10	d	a	b	c
11	b	d	a	c
My Score*	/8	/8	/8	/8

*Total the number of answers from each column

Your Martok-Singleton Player Type

Examine the totals in each of the columns: the highest number indicates your dominant playing style, the second highest is your auxiliary trait, and the other traits should be considered dormant. Pay particular attention to your dominant attribute, but read through the other descriptions to gain insight into the more subtle aspects of your playing style. No single trait is considered superior to another; however, in practice players will vary wildly in their ability to capitalize on their own strengths.

Aggressive

You are easily angered and will attempt to eliminate a perceived threat by striking quickly and decisively. During play you should strive toward taking an early lead and attempt to maintain your advantage throughout the match. Success will be achieved through the use of offensive strategies, intimidation, and a reliance on Rock-based gambits. The aggressive player usually has a few fairly obvious tells and must work hard to minimize the clues you give away to your opponents.

Spiritual

You trust your emotions. When competing, you focus on your own game, seeking inspiration from within and relying on inner harmony to select your throws. Winning or losing is not the primary focus of your game. Instead, you focus upon playing the right throw for any given situation, regardless of your opponent's actions. The spiritual player can usually benefit greatly from strategies that rely upon proper form and technique (such as cloaking and shadowing). The downfall of the spiritual player comes from being so inwardly focused that you fail to recognize an opponent's obvious mistakes.

Logical

Sound reasoning is the hallmark of a logical player. You have a knack for concentrating on the task at hand and the discipline to follow your vision to the end. Structured gambit play is an excellent way to plan your throws ahead of time. Counting your opponent's throws combined with pattern detection and avoidance strategies are solid choices for these players. However, strict adherence to preset strategies can leave you vulnerable to players with a more adaptive strategy.

Reactionary

The true strength of the reactionary lies in responding and adapting to your opponent's approach. You are naturally gifted at reading early warning signs from another player, so trust your instincts. Keep your options open during a match, and seek to adjust quickly to counter your opponent's tempo. The chief weakness of the reactionary player is often an inability to commit for long to a definite strategic direction. Be wary of overreacting to your opponent's moves since a skilled manipulator can often lead the reactionary player to ruin.

Knowing one's own type is vital to discovering what strategies are in line with personal strengths. The test can also be used with the purpose of profiling potential opponents to gain insight into their weaknesses. While this test has proven remarkably successful in helping novices develop their primary strengths, most advanced players use much more sophisticated self-assessment tools, which are outside the scope of this book.

RPS play can move beyond even advanced strategies into ever-higher forms of play. While Rock Paper Scissors is a game primarily of strategy, there is a weapon of even greater subtlety in the arsenal of the well-rounded player—meta-strategies, also known as gamesmanship.

6

GAMESMANSHIP

"Paper is the answer,
should Rock be the question."

C. Urbanus, player, referee,
and NE U.S. Classic organizer, 1998

GAMESMANSHIP:
THE GAME OUTSIDE THE GAME

What separates RPS from other sports is the extent to which gamesmanship is a factor in even the most casual play. RPS strategy is concerned with what occurs within the actual game, whereas gamesmanship concentrates more on positioning for victory. This may be accomplished by a few discouraging words to one's opponent or be a much more elaborate affair involving misdirection and acting. Gamesmanship relies heavily on the principle that "perception is reality" and that gaining the perceived advantage even when down will lead to success. Effective gamesmanship allows the player to deceive an opponent into making a predictable throw or have the opponent miscalculate one's next throw. While some of these strategies are considered heavy-handed, others require a much subtler touch. Whatever the strategy, the key to successful gamesmanship is never to let the opponent realize that he is being manipulated. It's critical to understand that gamesmanship does not cross the line into actual cheating since blatant cheating is never in style in RPS.

Priming the Chump
*Difficulty: ***

The purpose of priming is of course to get both players in synch to ensure a simultaneous delivery of throws.

Since the official speed of priming has never been established by the World RPS Society Steering Committee, nor is there any intention ever to rule on the issue, players possess the inherent right to dictate their own speed of play. This can be used to advantage when two players meet for the first time, since it is often unclear what the priming speed should be. The tendency is to default to the speed of the faster player. This allows the faster priming player the luxury of dictating the flow of play and causes the opponent (or "the chump") to dedicate more energy to "catching the prime" rather than concentrating on delivering an effective throw.

Should an opponent attempt this, the player would be well advised immediately to slow down the prime in order to force an out-of-synch situation. Making a comment to the opponent about his being a "little overexcited" and to "take it easy" is a nice touch to complete this counterstrategy and reestablish dominance for the rethrow.

Known counterstrategies: Sloth play

The Rusty Defense
Difficulty: *

This is not a recommended ploy and is frowned upon at most levels of play. The only reason for listing it here is to help the novice recognize when it is being used against him. The goal of this ploy (the term strategy does not apply here) is not to improve odds of winning, but instead to create a safety net for "Rusty"—the player who claims to be "out of practice" and who predicts his own defeat. This may put an opponent off his guard or may instill a false sense of confidence, but it rarely has a significant effect on a match. Still, some players swear by it and continue to include it in their repertoire.

It usually begins with an opponent claiming that he once played at a competitive level but has been out of practice or is rusty. The primary focus of this play is to sidestep the effects of losing games for honor. The rusty loser is then able to claim back some of his lost honor by regaling the winner with tales of his younger days or complaining about a fictitious bout of arthritis.

Should "Rusty" actually claim victory on the match, it enables him to boast twice the honor, for his ability to win despite being so out of practice. This invariably leads to confessions of "surprise" or comments such as "Rusty's still got it!" Most serious and conscientious RPS players eschew the use of the rusty defense, since keeping up with an RPS-training regimen is a cornerstone of competitive play at any level and can never be considered a valid excuse.

Known counterstrategies: None

Beware the wily old player who claims to be out of practice.

The Bait and Switch

*Difficulty: ***

This is a crowd-pleasing strategy that requires nerves of steel and control over reactive tendencies. There are many variations, but they all rely upon the principle of convincing an opponent that he has figured out the strategy only to switch strategies before completing the expected sequence.

The art of this strategy rests in utilizing false tells to help broadcast the perceived intention and mask the true one. The Scissors Sandwich gambit (PSP) illustrates this principle best. After a successful completion of the first Paper and second Scissors in the sequence, an opponent with even a rudimentary understanding of the game will suspect the last Paper to complete the tastiest of the Great Eight Gambits. By cleverly switching to another throw in the repertoire—such as Rock or Paper—a player can very easily prevail over the opponent.

Known counterstrategies: Sicilian reasoning

The Bait-and-Switch Switchback

*Difficulty: ****

A more complex variation of the bait and switch is to trick an opponent into expecting a bait and switch and then switch back to the original gambit. A typical debate with beginner RPS players is whether this strategy is anything more than the simple execution of the original gambit. In the case of the Avalanche gambit, it would appear so, since the player has technically executed the three requisite rocks. It is, however, this type of debate that separates the Rank Novice from the Professional, since a learned player understands that it is the thinking going on between each throw where the real game takes place. This is why at the higher levels of the sport, typical gambits such as the Avalanche are, despite appearances, rarely used. The three Rock throws are more likely to be Bait-and-Switch Switchbacks.

Known counterstrategies: Chaos play

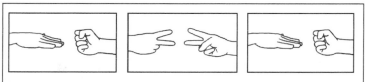

BAIT-AND-SWITCH SWITCHBACK. Note the remarkable resemblance to a Scissors Sandwich.

Applying Intimidation
Difficulty: Varied,
depending upon the confidence level of opponent

Bravado and other overt grandiloquent displays are typical of many RPS matches played at the professional level. It is precisely this type of display that provides the clearest departure from the battle of wits seen in chess. The general rule of intimidation is to get an opponent to doubt his own abilities, causing him to lose composure and become vulnerable to attack. Trash talking serves a dual purpose; vocally flaunting one's own skills will bolster one's own confidence in addition to unsettling the opponent by putting him down. Rob Krueger, winner of the 2003 Molson Canadian RPS World Championships, bludgeoned his competition using a variation of this technique. On each pump of the three primes he would bellow a ritualistic cadence of "Ro . . . Sham . . . Bo . . ." and then "BOOM" during his final approach. His approach was so effective that he didn't lose a single match during the entire competition.

One critical element for the trash-talking player is to

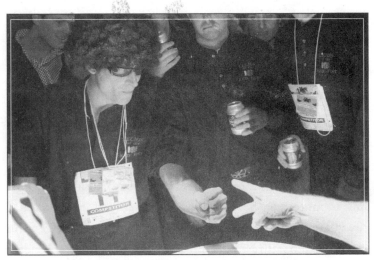

Rob Krueger, 2003 World RPS Champion *(left)* with teammates from Legion of the Red Fist surrounding him during qualifying play at the RPS World Championships. (Photo by Mark Coatsworth)

take advantage of each win in a series to further reinforce his dominance through continued verbal attacks usually focused on the opponent's poor play or the player's own superior RPS skills.

Known counterstrategies: Earmuffs

Double Speak

A good intimidation suggestion is to use lines that may be interpreted both literally and figuratively. For instance, if you threaten an already nervous opponent that you are going to "kick his butt," he will end up spending more time looking out for the threatened foot foul rather than concentrating on his throw. Or a suggestion that you will "clean his clock" will result in an opponent examining his watch face for embarrassing smudges.

Timing Time-Outs

Difficulty: **

When losing during an important match, a player may wish to call for a short time-out to regain his senses and composure. This serves a dual purpose: allowing the player to take stock of the situation, and, should his opponent be nervous, allowing the opponent to become even more tense and unbalanced. If a player has already used the last remaining time-out of the match, he can consider requesting a technical time-out for an equipment check. An untied shoe is perfect in this sense. Many players search for the longest laces they can find for the very purpose of being able to untie them at will with their other foot. Remember to use the time to get equipment back in tip-top shape, but do not appear to be delaying the game. If playing over a table, make sure to lace up under the table and away from view from the opponent. Being out of sight will unnerve an opponent further; the longer it takes to get equipment back in order, the more he will wonder what is going on under the table skirting. Being under the table also allows for a quick check of an opponent's shoes. If his shoes are also untied, or if he is wearing inappropriate footwear, pointing this out to him will make him feel that less in tune with the game. Furthermore, an untied lace for an opponent can be a signal that he is planning an equipment timeout of their own.

Known counterstrategies: Penny loafers

Crystal Ball
*Difficulty: ***

One of the more clever gamesmanship strategies, the crystal ball is a ploy to confuse an opponent and derail what might be an otherwise effective offensive strategy. To employ the crystal ball, forcefully declare—whether certain or not—what the opponent will play next:

"You're going to bring Scissors again, aren't you?"

If the opponent is unfamiliar with this ploy, he will not throw Scissors. That makes Paper a safe throw. Verbal authority is critical with this strategy so that the opponent does not think the player is simply using the less complex fishing strategy, in which a player merely asks what his opponent's next throw will be.

Known counterstrategies: Faithful servant, which involves confirming your opponent's belief by playing exactly what he says you will play.

The Surprise Game (or the Barlow Effect)
(Note: This strategy is meant to be used outside of tournament play.)
Difficulty: **

Often surprise can be a great tactic for winning lightning RPS bouts. An otherwise mediocre player, Sean Barlow, who spent years plugging in the middle ranks of the competitive semipro circuit, first perfected the surprise game strategy, or Barlow Effect. He was notorious for initiating his nontournament matches very quickly without giving his opponents time to think. In this deceptively simple-to-learn yet complex-to-master maneuver, planning and timing are the essential components. As with the best magic tricks, misdirection is required in order to achieve success. The best candidates on which to use this tactic are current, future, or past friends who are naturally excitable, impulsive, and always overly eager to play a match.

Simply ask someone for a quick game of RPS and,

before he even has time to answer, begin priming. By immediately beginning the priming phase before the opponent has a chance to react, the target's instinct will take over and he will do everything possible to catch the prime. In essence, this concept uses the priming-the-chump strategy as the beginning ruse, which can be applied with devastating results.

Once an opponent is in a reactionary mind-set, the player wins the game, providing his next move is Paper. Why? Nine times out of ten, under these conditions, the opponent will throw Rock. By catching the target off guard, he does not have time to begin thinking about a strategy. In this situation, the easiest move to play is Rock. The reason is twofold:

1. Playing rock requires the least displacement of digits, and, when caught off guard, an opponent does not have the time to play anything else.
2. Because playing Rock is considered an aggressive move, an opponent will erroneously assume that to compensate for his surprise he needs to come out strong.

Known counter strategies: Equipment check.

The RPS Magician
(or How to Meet Girls* with RPS)

Difficulty: Varied, depending upon player's attractiveness

Imagine the great fun to be had in meeting members of the opposite sex using the principles learned in the surprise game strategy. A variation of this play will allow one to impress anyone (friends or strangers) with dazzling playing ability and skills. The best place for this is often a crowded bar where there are lots of other distractions about.

First, scout out the intended victim, just as you do for the surprise game strategy. Then, before playing, find a group of patrons worth impressing. This works particularly well as an introduction to a group of females. Next, boast to the group about the quality of your RPS skills. In fact, they are so good that not only will you win the next game that you play, but you can tell them beforehand what the as-yet-to-be-named opponent will play (Rock). Imagine the disbelief that will result from such a bold statement of claim! Once the daring prediction has been made to the group, go up to the victim and use the surprise game strat-

---

*While girls could certainly employ this tactic to meet boys, we have found that it is rarely necessary for girls to have to go to these great lengths to meet guys for the simple reason that most guys are usually attracted to any girl who plays RPS. The best strategy for a girl wanting to meet guys with RPS is simply to walk up to an attractive male and ask for a game. An unattached male will rarely reject such a tempting offer.

egy. Remember to keep both hands in view so the audience can witness everything. With the ice successfully broken and the newfound friends duly impressed with your skills, remember the old magician's adage: "Never repeat a trick, and never tell them how it is done."

If the temptation to perform again is too strong, or if forced into a situation in which members of the audience see the trick twice, simply switch from telling them that the opponent will lose by playing Rock to telling them that a win will be achieved by playing Paper. Positioning the tactic in this way will shift the focus away from your delivering the same throw twice.

Known counterstrategies: Scissors.

The Wildman
Difficulty: ***

This strategy is the art of convincing an opponent that the wildman is a complete lunatic and therefore capable of truly random throws. However, be assured that this randomness is utterly feigned. The strategy can be recognized primarily by statements designed to make an opponent overconfident. They range from the subtle, such as "Don't look at me; I have no idea what I am doing" to the extreme, such as "There are bugs controlling my brain!" Imaginary friends, paranoid delusions, and hallucinations are frequently part of the act. It can be extremely demoralizing to lose to a wildman. This strategy should never be attempted by novices, since one must actually have an excellent grasp of strategy to succeed both in the game and in the deception. A rather ingenious twist is the use, by the wildman, of a sidekick, or "second," who will insist on behalf of the wildman just how wild and random the throws are.

Known counterstrategies: Crystal ball

The Old Hat
Difficulty: ***

The old hat simply acts as if he knows exactly what his opponent's next move will be by use of ruthless patronization. The purpose of this strategy is to demoralize an

"Rock would have been a better choice for you" is typical Old Hat banter.

opponent into feeling inferior or intimidated so he will make obvious mistakes in a blind panic to regain his composure. This strategy is equally compelling whether a paternal or maternal attitude is taken. Its effectiveness is minimized by the fact that nearly every player nowadays will recognize the "Ol' Old Hat."

Common "Old Hat" banter includes:

"Rock? Hmmm . . . Frankly, I am surprised that Paper didn't occur to you."

"This time, actually *think* before you throw."

"I don't suggest using the Avalanche gambit on me; I did invent it, after all."

"I *knew* that would be your next move."

Known counterstrategies: Lucky beginner

RUSTY VS. OLD HAT

Rarely in RPS do you see such an annoying combination of players as when you are forced to endure Rusty's wretched attempt to fly under the radar against the Old Hatter's ruthless one-upmanship. In fact, even being in the same room as these two players is generally considered too much for most observers.

Using Size Against an Opponent
Difficulty: ***

Since Rock is often interpreted as a display of physical strength, players who enjoy a large physical presence are often able to win a first-round match quickly through giving verbal cues that they have "nothing but Rock" on their mind, then coming out with Scissors to counter the expected response of Paper. Flexing of muscles and other obvious examples of knuckle-dragging behavior can easily dupe a less-experienced player into believing Rock is the only move in one's repertoire, or is at least the favored throw. A rise in popularity of this particular strategy has caused many players to undertake hazardous body-building programs concentrating on bulk rather than strength to bolster this image. In fact, steroid use has been increasing in the sport as a direct result of players looking to fit the stereotypical image of a Rock player.

Known counterstrategies: David and Goliath play—countering size with ingenuity

Tattoo Play
Difficulty: ****

Strategic placement of distracting body modifications can be highly effective in RPS tournaments. Metal piercings on the face or the hand can be subtle cues of a leaning toward throwing Scissors. Likewise, tattoos evoke thoughts of Paper in many opponents. Some players go a step further and actually get images or names of various throws tattooed on parts of their hand. For example, similar to prison tattoos, some players have been witnessed with the letters R, O, C, and K tattooed, one on each knuckle of their hand. (Note: Paper and Scissors do not work quite as well with this method. Should a player feel strong enough to want the word "scissors" tattooed on his knuckles, he can spread the eight letters across both hands.) Rest assured that any player who has gone to the trouble, pain, and expense of getting an RPS-themed body modification is likely to be a serious contender.

Known counterstrategies: Averted vision

Alden Greenhouse sports a subtle and temporary variation on Tattoo Play. This type of display, when used judiciously, devastates an opponent. (Photo by Kathy Maukner)

Spirituality
Difficulty: *****

Spirituality is a catchall phrase for all faith-based and fatalistic approaches to **RPS**. This includes organized religion, Eastern philosophies, and the entire gamut of crackpotism. While for some projecting an image of spirituality is as simple as wearing an obvious religious symbol, elaborate prayer rituals, demon summoning, and the wearing of numerous bells to frighten off evil **RPS** spirits have all been seen at pro-level matches. No matter what higher force the spiritual power emanates from, the trick is to convince an opponent that you are serious and perhaps even disturbed. The magic of spiritual play lies in the fact that one can never lose; one can only be the victim of a capricious deity. God may not play dice with the universe, but His **RPS** skills are unmatched.

Known counterstrategies: Heathenism

Playing the Referee
Difficulty: Varied, depending upon the referee

This strategy works best in tournament situations and utilizes the principle that no matter what the outcome of a called foul may be, one should always side with the referee. If the foul is called against the opponent, look disparagingly at him and then offer a knowing glance to the ref as well as an indignant expression, as if it is beneath a serious player to compete against such a vulgarian.

Should the call be in the opponent's favor, give the impression that you were simply testing the ability of the ref to make the right call and nod politely to the referee while looking at your opponent as if to say, "You could do to learn from this man." Even though most refs enjoy the position of power and the fleeting respect the position commands, strike a balance between being courteous and overtly sucking up to him. If the referee is wearing a name tag, feel free to use his given name.

To exaggerate the effect, prior to the start of the match casually ask the referee whether he has seen A. C. Billingsworth (or any other equally fictitious, yet convincing name) at this year's competition. Regardless of the answer, the opponent will assume that you and the ref share a long-standing friendship, or that you are more plugged in to the tournament circuit.

Known counter-strategies: Playing the grand marshal

Being the player to "watch out for" is central to my strategic approach. The key to keeping my opponent off his game is to control the game with what I call a distraction point. Therefore, my style of play is all about style. Picking the right outfit for a tournament forms the core of my strategy. I have found that against men, the most effective distraction point is cleavage, so I play my prime close to my chest in order to press this advantage. Lately on the professional circuit, I have noticed a sharp upturn in other women's use of the more subtle midriff exposure technique, but I am a traditionalist in my approach. I come from the "If you got it, use it" school of RPS. Despite what my stats may suggest, I would say that I am without a doubt the most successful player on the professional circuit, if you measure success by the size of one's endorsement contracts, which I of course do. I have taken a certain amount of flak for missing major tournaments that happen to conflict with outside obligations such as my "Jasmine Meade Rocks America" mall tour, but when you have the kind of endorsement contracts I have, there are certain obligations that you must meet. That is just a fact I have to deal with.

Professional-Level Play
and Etiquette

"My mum told me, 'Don't throw rocks,
don't play with scissors.' I'll bet you're
choking on those words now, eh, Mum?"

An excerpt from Dave Bradbury's victory speech
after winning 1943 UK Regionals (he was later
invited to join the legendary London All Browns)

Attendance at RPS tournaments is growing in popularity every day. Purses are getting larger, serving to raise the profile of the sport. Competitors are under a false assumption, however, if they feel that achieving a degree of success in pedestrian matches will prepare them for pro-circuit play. Placing well consistently at

RPS tournaments is exceptionally difficult. While sports like chess favor mental fortitude and others such as long-distance running emphasize physical abilities, RPS requires an immense amount of both qualities in order to achieve success. To place well at the pro level, one must enter a competition in prime physical and mental condition.

RITUALIZING THE WIN

Many amateur players engage in a form of RPS that has the winner of the match actually mimicking the real-life interactions of the RPS elements referred to as ritualizing the win. For example, upon playing Paper to best Rock, the player would actually slap their palm on the top of their opponent, or, far worse, attempt to physically crush an opponent's Scissors with their Rock.

It was once common practice during tournaments to ritualize the win, but unfortunately, for a promising young player, this practice proved disastrous. In a hotly contested semifinal round, Mustafa Nwenge of Kenya pulled Scissors and had the ligaments in his index finger violently torn as a result of an overzealous Rock by a Swedish contestant. Needless to say, the RPS Steering Committee banned the practice and instituted the no-contact rule for matches. Sadly, Mustafa was never able to play competitively again, but the society has received word that he is in very hot demand as a motivational speaker.

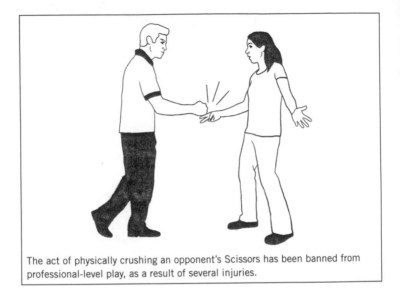

The act of physically crushing an opponent's Scissors has been banned from professional-level play, as a result of several injuries.

Pretournament Training

Nutrition

Many RPS players spend too much time worrying about what kind of and how much food they should eat prior to a competition. The World RPS Society advises players to stay away from fad diets, drink lots of fluids (preferably water), and consider brain foods such as fish. If fresh fish is too hard to find or catch, eat no more or less than a usual routine demands. The risks of rashly changing diet a few days before the competition outweigh any potential benefits.

Building Forearm Stamina

Tournament RPS requires players to play hundreds of individual games before the final match. Building forearm stamina is key to developing a good strong prime and being able to keep it up in the later rounds. An enjoyable exercise is to try continuous and repetitive motions with the arm in an up-and-down fashion. Although this exercise can be done literally anywhere, it is a technique best left for the privacy of the bedroom (a shower can make a good alternate choice). Be sure also to practice with the nondominant hand. Variety will not only keep motivation high during training sessions, but it will keep an alternate hand ready in case of an injury.

Videotapes

Wherever possible, examine videotapes of an opponent's matches. Study them closely and watch to see what strategies he relies upon in times of desperation or when he is pressing his advantage. Use slow-motion controls to look for any obvious tells or patterns. If a player's name is unknown, write down the bib number he is wearing and check this against one of the many Web sites that keep track of player standings.

To Practice or Not to Practice

Obviously practice is an important part of any training program, but there is considerable debate about the best way to get ready for a major tournament. Some players prefer crash-style training, which focuses on playing as many games as possible in the days leading up to the event. Others players call this method the crash-and-burn approach and insist that it causes one to peak too early. Many feel that abstaining from play entirely leading up to a major tournament not only reduces the possibility of injury but ensures well-rested muscles for the opening match.

TOURNAMENT PLAY

What to Expect

Each major tournament has its own unique ambiance and character. The Southwestern U.S. Pro-Am Invitational is held at the magnificent and serene Roshambo Vineyards in Healdsburg, California, and fosters a fairly laid-back style of play. Whereas, the annual World Championships, known for intense play and grandiose costumes, are held in large, open, and brightly lit facilities in urban locations. Many other tournaments are set everywhere from small bars and coffeehouses all the way to desert or mountain matches.

Getting a feel for the venue can also help an athlete in feeling comfortable during a match. If possible, seek out the building manager or custodian. They can be a wealth of site information, such as how the temperature of the venue charges based upon the number of expected players. Venues that use excessive air-conditioning can adversely affect play. Conversely, too much humidity can cause your limbs to swell, which can also slow down the general pace of play.

Locker Room Antics

The astute RPS player will gain advance knowledge of the tournament character and adapt his clothing, training regimen, and strategies accordingly. Should flight delays or conflicts not allow you to make a site inspection part of your pretournament regime, arrive early. This will allow you at least to secure a good location in the player's locker room. Pay no mind to any of the theatrical displays of the other players, who will often have elaborate and/or bizarre rituals whose only purpose is to unnerve less experienced players. As an example, Brett "the Detonator" MacLaren is known to bring his vast and menacing collection of scissors to every match, despite the fact that physical representations of the elements are strictly forbidden. He will slowly and methodically sharpen them in the locker room as a ploy to scare rookies. It is a widely accepted belief that the reason Brett has never placed well at a major tournament is because he is more focused on rattling the rookies rather than more experienced players.

Most players will be sniffing around for clues about

the competition, so discuss your tournament strategy in the locker room with a friendly stranger at your peril. This notion leads to the oft-quoted RPS aphorism: "The match is yielded before it begins to tongue waggers and knuckle draggers."

Lights, Cameras, Action!

The atmosphere when attending a major tournament for the first time can be unnerving. RPS tournaments attract top-tier media and tremendous spectator attention, so playing well under pressure separates the amateurs from

MEDIA CIRCUS. Professional player Master Roshambollah maintains composure amid an international media scrum. (Photo courtesy of Team All Too Flat)

the pros. What follows are some tips on how to ensure that you are at the top of your game in a tournament setting.

Dealing with the Crowd

Love them or hate them, crowds are here to stay at tournament-level RPS, not only at the match, but those at home watching the broadcasts as well. Remember:

GO PAPER! Spectator showing allegiance to a favorite throw.
(Photo by Mark Coatsworth)

"Crowds love, and crowds love to hate." Depending upon playing style and personality, one can capitalize on this. Some players enjoy playing the "bad boy" role and find that the more the crowd jeers at them the better they play. Other players prefer to label themselves the home-town hero (no matter how far they traveled) in an attempt to get the local crowd to support them.

RPS AS AN OLYMPIC SPORT?

Often players wonder if all their years of practice and training could be parlayed into Olympic Gold Medal dreams should the sport ever become part of the Olympics. The World RPS Society is very clear and firm on its view that RPS has no place in the world of Olympic sports. Wojek Smallsoa sums up the situation brilliantly: "RPS will never be an Olympic event. Considering the doping scandals and judging fiascos, RPS is much too honorable, and putting us in that lot will do nothing but disparage the reputation of our great sport."

Making an Entrance

By far the most popular opening strategy at major tournaments is to walk in like you are the one to beat. This can be accomplished by arriving in a limo, being accompanied by groupies (and/or an entourage), wearing outlandish attire, or many other attention-grabbing techniques. There are other more subtle but no less effective methods available. 2002 World RPS Champion Pete Lovering entered the World Championships sport-

Perennial World Championship host Michael Booth shows the crowd Pete Lovering's trademark bathrobe proclaiming his 1974 and 2002 victories. (Photo by Mark Coatsworth)

ing a green bathrobe proclaiming him to be the 1974 World Champion. Was this puffery on his part? Perhaps, but it obviously had the intended effect on each of his opponents as he went on to become world champion.

Winning the Media Game but Losing the Real Game

Pandering too much to the media at a major tournament is the downfall of many ambitious players. Often the ones who have little experience with the media will unwittingly share critical strategic insights before a match. Smart players hold back and listen as major players are interviewed, waiting for clues that may expose tournament strategies.

Some of the better-known players intentionally lay down red herrings with the media in prematch interviews. They will make rash pronouncements—such as "Rock is for rookies"—in the hope that potential opponents within earshot will erroneously assume that they will be favoring Scissors.

Whom Can You Trust?

The number-one rule at any RPS tournament is to trust no one but the referee. A competitor who looks and acts like a beginner may very well be a grizzled veteran disguising years of professional training with the intention of catching intermediate players off guard. This technique has recently become popular since many tournaments are moving to an open format, which allows novice players to compete.

Other players use more devious tactics. Professional competitor Rui Torrao has become notorious for entering tournaments with an arm in a sling in order to dupe players into believing he can compete only with his less-effective nondominant hand. At the most opportune moment, he will remove the sling and switch to his dominant hand, thereby unnerving his opponent.

Rui Torrao *(right)* playing switch with his "injured" right arm in a sling. Note the size difference of these two competitors. (Photo by Mark Coatsworth)

How to Act Like a Professional Even If You Are Not

Professionals project an image of composure and confidence. Even when not a true professional, many players choose to act like pros so that they will be treated like pros. Tournaments attract circuit players, so time and again the same faces will appear. But RPS has always been a meritocracy. With enough natural ability and/or skill, a player can literally come out of nowhere to win a competition.

In order to project credibility, a player must first establish credentials outside the competition arena. Side games are particularity effective places to earn renown.

Seek out side-game challenges with players of a higher stature; players of a lower rank will do nothing to build your reputation. If a player can claim a few wins off some of the higher-ranking competitors, word that there is a hot new player will spread quickly.

Be forewarned that it is not easy to convince a circuit player of higher rank to play someone of lower rank. Many high-level players refuse to play side games during a competition. With a combination of taunts, friendly insults, and poultry references, one may coax a game from a well-respected competitor. For the challenger, it is a no-lose situation. A win results in immediate respect, a loss will result in admiration for having had the guts to confront a better player. There is no shame in losing to a superior player.

Be skeptical of players who claim to have won tournaments with which you are unfamiliar. Often players will claim to be a finalist at a tournament such as the annual "Bali High Open." They may even produce a newspaper article with a photo of their "win" as proof. Keep in mind that for a small sum, local counterfeiters in Bali will produce fake newspaper articles with any supplied photograph claiming a win at the tournament.

Other players have been known to ride an ancient tournament success. A quick reply of "You are only as good as your last tournament placing" is usually enough to put the has-beens in their place.

Playing the Numbers
(or the Secret of Teams)

RPS tournaments have a lot in common with political conventions. Once a contender has been eliminated, he will seek to swing his support to another competitor. The best way to ensure a higher profile in competitive-level play is to join a team or, better yet, to start a team and elect yourself captain. In the case where the captain is knocked out early, he can still cheer on the team members as they make their way to the final rounds. Should a teammate make it to the finals and win, the team captain will be able to boast about the team's overall performance. This will give those willing to listen the impression that the captain taught the player everything he knows or that, at the very least, it was the captain's eye that spotted such an incredible talent.

DEALING WITH AN UNEXPECTED MOVE BY YOUR OPPONENT

Despite your best preparations for a major tournament, an opponent may still completely blindside you with an unexpected throw such as Scissors when you were sure Rock was coming. Faced with this situation, remember that you have three basic options for responding to anything your opponent throws at you:

A. Ignore it and keep on strategy.
B. Appear to ignore it yet subtly shift strategies.
C. Overtly modify your response.

There is only one rule for deciding which option to use and how to shape your specific response, and that rule is that there is no rule. Remember that and you will do fine.

TOURNAMENT ETIQUETTE

Tournament etiquette today differs greatly from that in the 1920s. Few current players continue to respect the old traditions of formal attire and elaborate forms of address. As a game of honor, higher standards of conduct are demanded of the RPS player, both inside and outside of the arena. However, the following general guidelines are still considered appropriate behavior for tournament-level play:

Players

★ All players must appear at their starting time and ideally several minutes before to perform a final equipment check.

★ A player should never consult or accept unsolicited information from a spectator. If this information is offered, the player should ignore it.

★ Players should not cause unnecessary delays. In extreme cases delaying tactics may result in a penalty.

★ While lighthearted verbal jockeying and jousting is permitted between players during the match, hurling insults and epithets is considered bad form and may be penalized by the referee.

★ Players should note that in the absence of a referee both players become referees-in-common and as such are entitled to discuss game status and rule clarifications. Any disputes arising between the coreferees shall be resolved via RPS.

★ All players should be familiar with the Player's Responsibility Code.

★ Upon conclusion of the game, it is considered good form to acknowledge an adversary's presence, although a handshake is considered superfluous.

★ RPS is a game without ties, so whether one wins or loses, conducting oneself with good grace is absolutely necessary.

Spectators

★ Spectators must refrain from making audible comments on the proceedings.

★ Spectators need to abstain from any unnecessary movement within the players field of view, such as excessive hand waving.

★ Spectators should never offer advice to competitors or draw attention to a player's bungled strategy.

★ Photographers, camera operators, journalists, and groupies must allow sufficient room for players to maneuver.

Tournament Format Best Three of Three

Generally all sanctioned World RPS events follow a best three-of-three format. This means that winning a best-two-out-of-three set will earn one point, and a player will need to win two points to move on to the next round. Two winning throws earns a set. Two winning sets earns the match. In other words, you must win two best-of-three sets to move forward. This game-set-match style of RPS is preferred over a straight best-of-seven or -nine format because it allows players, when a set is lost, to put the loss behind them and begin the next set with a fresh perspective.

OFFICIAL RPS PLAYING AIDS AND ACCESSORIES

As with most sporting activities and pastimes, playing aids and accessories always seem to become a point of interest among keen players. RPS is no exception. Even though RPS can be enjoyed without any equipment, there have been many products developed to enhance training and game play.

Official World RPS Players Log: A must for the player who wants to keep track of game play. This seven-hundred page logbook keeps track of more than fifteen thousand individual games. It is considered standard equipment for both novice and professional-level players. Consider ordering this product in tandem with the Official World RPS Players Log-Carrying Device for easy transportation of this tome.

Note: The Log-Carrying Device replaces the formerly available Log-Carrying Contraption, which has been recalled as a result of a dangerous design flaw. Players who still use the contraption should keep children and pets away from it at all times and return it to the point of purchase immediately.

Official World RPS Three-Fingered Training Glove: This glove has been developed with the professional player in mind. Reinforced material in the index and middle fingers trains the player to deliver a quicker Scissors release. Since the pinky and ring finger are not needed for play, sleeves for those two have been combined for greater ease and comfort.

Official World RPS Portable Arena: 4 X 4 feet all-weather wooden playing area complete with foot position markings allows players to achieve the feeling of tournament play in their own backyard. Also available is a roll-up version for easier storage and transport or for play on the road. For added realism, include the Official World RPS Blow-Up Ref Doll, which comes preprogrammed with action phrases such as "Players ready?" "Throw!," and "Watch your form!"

Official World RPS Plush Toys: Soft toys to cuddle and spread love for the game among children. Three varieties to choose from: Rocky the Rock, Peter Paper, or Sally Scissors. An ideal way to get young children interested in the game.

Official World RPS Sweatbands: Can be used for tournament play, marathon matches, or any time when heat is a factor.

Framed Players Responsibility Code (PRC): Nothing looks better above a shelf full of RPS trophies than this item. Hand-printed on real parchment paper, the PRC is signed by Wojek Smallsoa, who, at the time when the code was developed, was in charge of the World RPS Standards and Best Practices Committee.

HOW TO LEARN
ABOUT UPCOMING TOURNAMENTS

Dozens of tournaments are held throughout the world. Some tournaments are sanctioned by the World RPS Society, while other rogue tournaments do not necessarily adhere to the World RPS Society standards. To keep abreast of tournaments taking place, simply visit the World RPS Society's Web site at worldrps.com.

8

GAME VARIATIONS

"I can get on a bus in just about any city in the world and play for the last remaining seat without speaking a word. RPS is truly the world's most popular game."

Professor Tyson Howell,
associate professor of comparative folklore,
World RPS Society Educational Brigade

The game of RPS has been passed from generation to generation, neighborhood to neighborhood, and country to country. No other game in the world enjoys as much cultural diversity as RPS. The World RPS Society celebrates the differences of these minor cultural variations in casual play, provided that the tripartite principles of the game are preserved. However, none of these variations are permitted in tournament situations. Chairman Wojek Smallsoa is fond of paraphrasing Chairman Mao on the matter: "Letting a hundred flowers blossom and a hundred schools of thought contend is the policy for promoting the progress of game."

So it matters not if the game in one's neighborhood goes by the name Roshambo, Jan Ken Pon, Kai Bai Bo, or Ching Chong Chow. Nor does it matter if decisions are made not with Rocks, Paper, and Scissors but instead with Elephants, Humans, and Ants. What is important is that an RPS-based system is used to help settle, quickly and impartially, life's everyday disputes. While accepted for personal disputes, it is worthwhile to note that making the Elephant hand symbol will not be viewed with a tolerant eye on the pro circuit. This chapter will examine other variations in the way the game is played, including multiplayer games.

CULTURAL VARIATIONS OF RPS

The World RPS Society made a significant investment in Internet technology in 1995 in order to foster the largest RPS intracultural study to date. The information garnered by the World RPS Society's ORiGIN Task Force was not limited to the invention of the game, it also created the largest list to date of RPS name variations. Generally, the different names of the game follow one of two distinct patterns:

1. Element-based variations translated directly from the physical representations such as Roche Ciseaux Papier, which in French is literally Rock Scissors Paper.
2. Vocalized rhythmic cadences using nonsense words that are generally indicative of the vocalizations players use while engaging in the priming ritual such as Ching Chong Cha.

Known **RPS** name variations from around the world:

Ching Chang Chong (Germany)
Ching Chong Cha (South Africa)
Chinging (United Kingdom)
Fargling (United States)
Guu Choki Paa (Japan)
Jan Ken Po (Hawaii)
Janji (Thailand)
Janken or Jan Ken Pon (Japan)
Kai Bai Bo (Korea)
Muk Chi Baa (Indonesia and Korea)
One Two Three (Vietnam)
Paper Scissors Stone (United Kingdom)
Pierre Feuille Ciseaux (France)
Roche, Ciseaux, Papier (Quebec, Canada)

Roshambo (United States)

Schnik-Schnak-Schnuck (Germany)

Most countries generally adopt a few names, but nowhere are the variations more densely packed than in London. Names such as Ching Chang Cholly (South London), Chu Chin Chow (Enfield), Ick Ack Ock (Croydon), Eee Pas Vous (Lambeth), and Stink Stank Stoller (Brixton) are all able to coexist peacefully within a single city.

Some name variations even provide interesting clues into how the game initially migrated to or developed in the area. For example, Hawaii enjoys a large community of Japanese émigrés. Hawaiians call the game Jan Ken Po, which is an obvious adaptation from the Japanese Jan Ken Pon. In Vietnam, it is likely that the game adopted the English name "One, Two, Three" during the 1970s when American servicemen were frequently encountered. It is now well known that the Vietnamese children were masters of the game and would routinely fleece visitors by pretending never to have played before.

THROW VARIATIONS

While the World RPS Society prefers to unite the world under the single banner of Rock Paper Scissors, the game is often played with unfamiliar throws (or even facial gestures) replacing the trinity. As a comparison, a similar situation arises in chess. A trip to any local gaming shop will provide a window into a world where novelty chess sets are based on characters from cartoons, science fiction, or samurai or war themes. As long as the rules remain intact, there is no harm in using these variations. One would be hard-pressed to see a Garry Kasparov competing in major chess tournaments wielding *Simpsons*-themed chess pieces, and for similar reasons alternate throw systems at sanctioned RPS tournaments are not permitted.

While most Western countries played with the traditional Rock, Paper, and Scissors format, the following chart lists several of the more popular Asian throw variation:

ASIAN THROW VARIATIONS			
COUNTRY/REGION	**THROW 1**	**THROW 2**	**THROW 3**
Japan	Headman	Gun	Fox
Japan	Hero	Tiger	Mother
Japan	Snake	Frog	Slug
Japan	Fire	Snake	Water
Japan	Hera	Spear	Nikko
Japan	Purse Lips	Stick Out Tongue	Open Mouth Wide
Japan	Put Legs Together	Cross Legs	Spread Legs
Okinawa	Tree	Bird	Insect
Japan	Father	Mother	Child

COUNTRY/REGION	THROW 1	THROW 2	THROW 3
China	Hammer	Scissors	Bomb
Indonesia	Elephant	Human	Ant
Korea	Rock	Scissors	Cloth
Singapore	Stone	Dragon	Water
Vietnam	Hammer	Nail or Scissors	Wrapping
Myanmar	General	Pistol	Surrender
Laos	Rock	Scissors	Paper
Malaysia	Rock	Bud or Beak	Well

Chart courtesy of Benjamin Peterson

Note: There are also many forms of the game that involve four throws or more. These have not been included because such atrocities violate the principles of the World RPS Society.

GAME VARIATIONS

Corporal Punishment RPS

One of the most common features of today's school-yard games is unbridled violence, and the once innocent game of RPS is not immune to this trend. A particularly barbaric mutation of RPS exists in the suburban underworld of public schools. The loser of a superficially innocent match of RPS must suffer the grueling physical torture and indignation of getting slapped on the underside of the forearm. In some cases the winner will be so sadistic that he will actually resort to licking his fingers prior to initiating the slap—moist fingers generate extra stinging power. While the forearm slap has been successfully eradicated in pro-circuit play, it is still common at the intramural and varsity levels of the sport.

The World RPS Society has taken a firm stance against this practice on the grounds that RPS is about rewarding the winner and not punishing the loser. The society has deployed the RPS outreach program with a mobile van to patrol school yards in an attempt to combat this alarming trend, but the proponents of this practice have gone underground and continue to evade detection. The society would like to encourage those who have become involved in this brutal netherworld to seek immediate treatment for their physiological and psychological injuries.

CORPORAL PUNISHMENT RPS. This barbaric postgame ritual is often executed with wet fingers for added sting.

Street RPS

If Corporal Punishment RPS drags the most high-minded of sports through the mud, Street RPS submerges the game in sewage. This ugly cousin of tournament play is engaged predominantly in the bowels of major metropolitan centers as a gambling activity. Readers of a gentle disposition will no doubt be offended by the notion that street urchins have corrupted the game by playing for money, cigarettes, and drugs. The World RPS Society has encouraged all players to keep away from this activity, not only for moral reasons but for safety concerns. The game itself can be characterized by a lack of referees and fast primes; the former causes frequent disputes, and the latter results in numerous injuries.

The practitioners of this activity often congregate in what are known as "fight clubs," where entrants pay a fee, and the winner of the competition takes the purse. Sources sympathetic to the World RPS Society indicate that these matches are often fixed; the organizers will fly in an out-of-town ringer who will prey on the ignorance and desperation of the locals. David Chant, a notorious Street RPS player who recently mended his ways after the birth of his first child, summarized the brutal dichotomy of winning such a match: "High-stakes Street RPS is a winner-take-all situation and attracts the most unsavory of characters. Let me ask you this: Do you re-

STREET RPS. Two unsavory ruffians play RPS for money.

ally want to be the only one holding a thousand bucks in a room full of broke crooks?"

STRIP RPS

RPS can be a great way to bring couples together or to inject a little variety and excitement into a mundane relationship. Strip RPS is played in the same way as normal RPS; of course the decision becomes who will remove an item of clothing. Play is repeated until one player has lost all clothing, and that player becomes the loser. Once a winner is declared, he or she has the option (although not the obligation) of removing any of his or her remaining clothes.

Handicap variation: In order to level the playing field should one player be much better than the other, the less-experienced player can make use of extra clothes such as an old overcoat or earmuffs. Note: Mittens should never be used as an extra piece of clothing as the player sporting them will have great difficulty in executing a Scissors throw.

MULTIPLAYER VARIATION

Rock Paper Scissors is the ideal way to make decisions between two people, but often decisions must be made between more than two people. At first glance RPS might seem an odd choice, but there are several methods that allow games with three or more players. Multiplayer games can be very challenging to navigate strategically and frequently require a scorekeeper.

Elimination

In this style of game, players form a circle and throw simultaneously according to the regular rules of RPS. If all three throws are present, a circular stalemate has occurred and a rethrow is required. If only two throws are present, then all players with the losing throw are eliminated from the game. The remaining players play again according to the same system. Players continue to be eliminated until only one player, the winner, remains. In

A group of players demonstrate the "elimination" multiplayer variation.

the case in which a loser must be selected for an undesirable task, the system is reversed. All players play together with the winners of each round removed and thus no longer eligible for the task. The chief drawback with this style of play is the propensity toward frequent stalemates, particularly among larger groups.

Points

The points-based game is ideal for assigning priority in a large group of people. All players throw simultaneously, and players gain a point for every losing throw played by an opponent. For example a group of four players deliver two Rocks, a Paper, and a Scissors. The Rock players each get one point (for beating the single Scissors), the Paper player gets two points (one for beating each Rock), and the Scissors player gets one point (for beating the Paper). The game continues until a preestablished score is reached.

Double Fisting

In this game players are arranged in a circle, and each plays simultaneously against both the player on his right and his left, using both hands. A player who loses to the throws on both sides is eliminated. When a player is eliminated, the circle reforms until only two players remain, at which time a regular match of RPS is played to declare the winner. Double fisting usually requires a referee; it is fairly easy for an unscrupulous player to take advantage of another's split attention and falsify his throws.

Attchi, Muite Hoy! (or Hey, Look Here!)

This particular variant, popular in Japan, uses standard RPS as a basis for the game, then adds in finger-pointing at the end of each RPS match. Two players play a regular game of RPS, and instead of declaring a winner and loser, the winning player will immediately say, *"Attchi, muite hoy!,"* and at the cry of *"hoy"* point one of his index fingers up, down, right, or left. The losing player will simultaneously point his or her head in one of these four directions. Should the losing player turn his face in the same direction in which the finger is pointing, play then

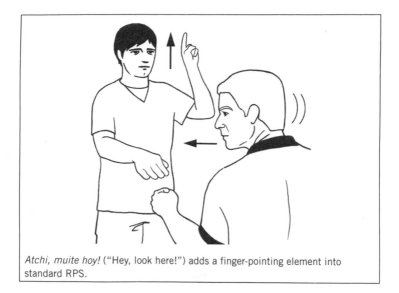

Atchi, muite hoy! ("Hey, look here!") adds a finger-pointing element into standard RPS.

stops and that player is declared the loser. If the directions do not match, then the players go back to playing another round of RPS. The process is repeated until a player is declared the loser. The game is played in rapid-fire fashion with players going from RPS to finger pointing and back without delay.

While none of the variations listed above are featured on the pro circuit, they are alternatives that have received the blessing of the World RPS Society for casual play. For some, however, the variations listed above do not satisfy their gluttonous ambitions and they crave delving into forbidden and illegal throws.

9

DYNAMITE AND
OTHER ILLEGAL THROWS

"She doesn't play any illegal throws
or anything. It is the way she plays
her throws that should be illegal."

Jef Hallestone, on Jasmine Meade
(cleavage-sporting 1998 National Junior Women's
Champion and author of *The Grrrls Guide to RPS*)

Rock Paper Scissors has been plagued over the years by countless attempts to "improve" the game beyond the basic trinity by adding a fourth and sometimes even a fifth throw. The World RPS Society Theoretical Throws Bureau has developed a special fast-track process for dealing with any other proposed four-throw systems, which involves the immediate filing of the proposal in the trash. The reasons for adding unnecessary complexity to an already perfect system are utterly incomprehensible and therefore easily dismissed. Experimenting with illegal throws is highly discouraged, and during tournament play engaging in them is grounds for immediate disqualification.

The Theoretical Throws Bureau has done yeomen service in discrediting every new throw to appear over the years. The World RPS Society's mission statement specifically mentions preserving the true game for future generations. However, no illegal throw has tested the patience of the society more than the tenacious throw of Dynamite.

THE MYTH OF DYNAMITE EXPOSED

The debate over the existence of Dynamite has probably been the single most heated discussion for novice players. The Dynamite hand gesture is formed with a closed fist and the thumb extended upward, or a "thumbs-up" motion.

The Theoretical Throws Bureau of the World RPS Society has a clear position: **Dynamite is incompatible with the Rock, Paper, and Scissors trinity.** The answer lies in simple logic. Compare these tables:

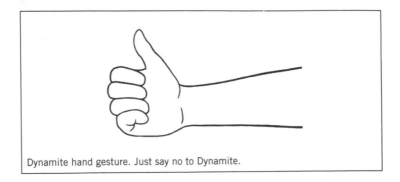

Dynamite hand gesture. Just say no to Dynamite.

CLASSIC RPS

	ROCK	PAPER	SCISSORS
ROCK	Tie	Paper wins	Rock wins
PAPER	Paper wins	Tie	Scissors wins
SCISSORS	Rock wins	Scissors wins	Tie

RPS WITH DYNAMITE ELEMENT

	ROCK	PAPER	SCISSORS	DYNAMITE
ROCK	Tie	Paper wins	Rock wins	Dynamite explodes Rock
PAPER	Paper wins	Tie	Scissors wins	???
SCISSORS	Rock wins	Scissors wins	Tie	Scissors snips the wick
DYNAMITE	Dynamite explodes Rock	???	Scissors snips the wick	Mutual destruction

Despite years of research, no one has developed a compelling argument regarding the result of a meeting between Dynamite and Paper. The leading opposing theories include the unwieldy "Paper snuffs out wick" or the preposterous "Wick burns through Paper." The World RPS Steering Committee has not ruled on the issue. In fact, the decision has been successfully postponed for more than thirty years, because to rule on the outcome of the Dynamite/Paper union could be interpreted as a tacit inclusion of this element in the sport. Even today it remains the most divisive issue in theoretical RPS. Should the issue ever actually be decided one way or the other, the result would certainly be explosive, as it would completely change the dynamic of the game. Inclusion of Dynamite, or any other four-throw deviation, is utterly illogical.

Dynamite also presents significant issues from a purely statistical perspective. Inclusion of this element would result in a throw that potentially loses more often than it wins, or vice versa. Either way it can be considered an unmitigated disaster. Furthermore, it would change the very nature of the other elements by making Rock a loser more often than a winner and Scissors a winner more often than a loser. Singlis Martok, the former World RPS executive vice chair of the Theoretical Throws Bureau and a well-known Dynamite opponent, is still the most often quoted source for the anti-Dynamite faction:

The misconception of Dynamite still hangs above RPS games like a great Death's Head, forcing otherwise reasonable RPS players into a whirling vortex of circular arguments. Let it be known that the World RPS Society does not now nor has it ever condoned the use of Dynamite in professional matches.

PARTIAL LIST OF ILLEGAL THROWS

New throws appear at an alarming rate. Many would-be game creators, in their haste to replace or expand upon the flawless trinity, abandon all semblance of good sense in the process. In some cases the added throws are so ridiculous and unbalanced that restrictions must be placed upon their use. In the case of throws like Fire and God, the intent is that they may be thrown only once in a lifetime, although how this directive could possibly be enforced is a mystery. The proponents of these absurd elements have not even taken the care to set up a registry to record when various players have employed a throw with such restrictions. One can never know for certain whether an unscrupulous player used his once-in-a-lifetime throw on another occasion. Or perhaps the throw was used while practicing in the shower. Would that count as a use? One can readily see the issues regarding this breed of illegal throws.

Some of the more prevalent illegal throws are listed below. Note: The discussion of illegal throws within this guide should not be considered in any way an acceptance of the legitimacy of these throws, nor should the exclusion of a throw from this list constitute any unwritten tolerance of that throw. They are listed purely to alert the novice player to the chicanery that they may experience in amateur play.

Devil and God

Devil hand gesture: Middle and ring finger curled inward, with index and pinky finger pointing up, thumb extended sideways.

God hand gesture: Full arm extended upward toward heaven with open palm.

In prior days, the Devil hand gesture was frequently encountered at heavy-metal concerts, but over the last decade, this evil throw has snaked its way into RPS. The throw is used as part of a five-throw system, along with another mythical throw known as God. According to legend, the Devil throw was developed as a defense against the God throw, which beats Rock, Paper, and Scissors. The God is a restricted throw and available to a player only once in a lifetime. Arguments about whether God or Devil triumphs in this system are not within the purview of this book and are best left to theologians.

Fire and Water

Fire hand gesture: Fingers and thumb pointing upward and flickering like a flame.

Water hand gesture: Palm flat and facing upward, with fingers wiggling like waves.

This five-throw system is as pointless as the God/Devil variant and suffers from similar logic inconsistency. At a sufficient temperature, Fire will melt Rock and Scissors, consume Paper, and can be extinguished by Water. In turn, at the hand of water, Paper becomes soggy, Rock sinks, and Scissors are rusted. Thus, Water is an unparalleled throw, negating the purpose of attempting any other throw.

Lightning

Lightning hand gesture: Index finger extended and pointing down.

The World RPS Society has uncovered numerous references to Lightning, but to date the society has exposed no useful clues as to how precisely the throw fits into the game. It appears to be part of a four-throw system bolted onto RPS. Like Dynamite, this unbalances the trinity and guarantees that one throw will win more often than it loses, or lose more often than it wins. This throw is believed to have been inspired by spectacular lightning strikes witnessed at the Cathedral Peak Resort in the

Drakensberg Mountains of South Africa, during the Natal RPS Regional in 1944.

Spock and Lizard

Spock hand gesture: Palm vertical and facing opponent with wide gap between middle and ring fingers. Also known as the "Live long and prosper" hand gesture.

Lizard hand gesture: Fingers pointing toward opponent with thumb brought underneath fingers, i.e., the "Sock Puppet" hand gesture.

Rock Paper Scissors Spock Lizard is one of the more recent developments in five-throw games, and to its credit it has the necessary internal symmetry to make for a playable game. However, due to the unnecessary complexity of the game, the World RPS Society continues to outlaw its use by card-carrying members. No doubt the element of Spock was added to reflect the logical nature of the game, but the relevance of Lizard has escaped society researchers.

The added throws are resolved as follows.

★ *Spock is poisoned by Lizard and disproved by Paper.*
★ *Spock vaporizes Rock and crushes Scissors (although how is uncertain).*
★ *Lizard is crushed by Rock and beheaded by Scissors.*
★ *Lizard poisons Spock and eats Paper.*

While the whimsical nature of the game may appeal to those of an infantile disposition, display of the Vulcan sign of peace and prosperity at any serious RPS tournament will likely result in quick ejection from the venue.

Texas Longhorn

Texas Longhorn hand gesture: Index, middle, and ring fingers curled inward, with thumb and pinky finger spread apart widely.

This throw is most common in the Southwest. The Longhorn is a representation of a bull's horns, and like many fourth throws, it "beats everything." Unlike many other throws, there appears to be no restriction on its use, begging the question why anyone would ever throw anything else. This turns an unreasonable four-throw game into a hollow one-throw game.

Note: Another Texas favorite is called the Mushroom Cloud, which, predictably, also beats everything. Deviant proponents of the throw have repeatedly petitioned the society to rename the game RPS&M.

The Bird

Bird hand gesture: Fist closed, with middle finger extended upward.

The Bird is actually not intended to be an additional throw in the game of RPS, but instead it sometimes appears as a response to a particularly bitter loss. It is listed here primarily because its use during a match in tournament play is grounds for the loss of one point at minimum. The most common response by an opponent who is the recipient of the Bird is the rapid delivery of a series of Rocks.

The Well

The Well hand gesture: Hand held palm up with fingers spread apart slightly and pointed upward.

Fringe players have proposed the Well to replace Rock as a solution to the question of how Paper beats Rock. The theory is that Scissors would sink in the Well and Paper would float on the water of the well. The Theoretical Throws Bureau is quick to point out the preponderance of dry wells, so there is no guarantee a well would have sufficient water in it. Besides, even whispers of replacing the beloved Rock with another element would be sure to cause massive worldwide protests.

Keeping abreast of all of the latest illegal throws can be a difficult task for anyone, so upon encountering an unknown throw, please contact a local chapter of the World RPS Society for more information. The rule of thumb when faced with an unknown or potentially illegal throw is to ask whether the throw can be identified as either Rock, Paper, or Scissors. If not, consider it an illegal throw.

10

Setting Up Clubs and Tournaments

"I believe in firmness, compassion,
and fair play. . . ."

Chuck "Stripes" Swalla, 1957 Championship referee

Playing RPS alone is pretty dull. Moreover, after learning the techniques in this book, outsmarting novice opponents will become fairly easy. The true beauty of RPS is in playing against many different players who each has his own unique style. RPS players are notoriously social, so the best way to attract players is with other players. Creating an RPS-friendly environment will draw players from all over. This chapter walks potential organizers and referees through the process of setting up a local RPS club, small tournament, or even a chapter of the World RPS Society, including the dos and don'ts of organizing tournaments, whether minor matches or World RPS–sanctioned events.

STARTING A LOCAL CLUB

The sport of RPS is growing. Every year legions of curious amateurs provide easy pickings for the more seasoned players on the pro circuit. So the need has never been greater for local RPS clubs to service the novice's thirst for competition and need for knowledge. However, with educational facilities facing tighter budgets, we can no longer count on the public infrastructure to fund local clubs or educate young prodigies. It is up to people like you, and we commend you for your desire to help.

RPS clubs provide:

★ *opportunities to play competitive RPS*
★ *A place to learn and develop better RPS skills*
★ *A sense of good sportsmanship*
★ *A support system when victory proves elusive*
★ *A focal point for community activity*
★ *A willing audience to listen to gloating over tournament victories*

The founding organizer of the club is expected to find a space where players can meet, then facilitate training, recruit new members, organize leagues or tournaments, and preside over club meetings. One of the great benefits of starting an RPS club is that no equipment needs to be purchased, thus costs can be kept very low.

RPS in the School System

The educational system has been resistant to providing RPS with the varsity sport designation it so rightly deserves. The society suspects a hidden motive is at hand. Consider the facts:

1. Middle and high school math teachers are infamous for using RPS to teach probability.
2. Designating RPS as a varsity or intramural sport would call into question the validity of using RPS in probability theory.

Therefore, the teaching community is attempting to preserve the status quo by remaining resistant to varsity RPS programs.

Q.E.D.

While the World RPS Society continues to lobby on behalf of students to include RPS as an officially designated school sporting program, there is nothing that limits students from establishing RPS through the back door of the school system by registering as a club. Follow this easy, step-by-step guide, and there should be no trouble in starting an RPS club in even the most oppressive academic atmosphere:

1. Find out about the necessary administration approvals and whether a faculty sponsor is required before the club is started.

2. When resistance is encountered from the administration, create a petition and collect enough signatures to convince those in authority of the need for an RPS club.

3. When the petition is inevitably rejected, do not despair. Simply be vocal about exhorting the benefits of game's conflict-resolution properties and openly accuse the administration of oppressing the rights of students. Talk up this injustice with anyone willing to listen, particularly yearbook and school newspaper staff. Should the rally leader have access to a megaphone, this will allow him to speak louder than any opponents.

4. At this point, the administration will refuse any and all discussion of the matter. This is a signal to kick the program into high gear. Pass out flyers and encourage the student body at large to support a school-wide protest. Students love to get involved in demonstrations regardless of the cause, so there should be no trouble getting the student body out in full force. If there is someone in your group

who is considered popular, consider making him a "celebrity" spokesman for the cause. Doing so will ensure a good turn out.

5. A good protest will always be more effective with catchy slogans on signs and clever rhyming chants, so supply these for the rally. If in a small town, contact the local newspaper, which is indubitably starved for real news, with advance notice of the demonstration. Victory is now at hand, since the administration will realize that it does not have sufficient reason to ban the club and, in an effort to try to salvage its flagging reputation, will reluctantly agree to sanction the club. Congratulations!

Junior RPS-sters

Younger children will often spontaneously organize their own RPS clubs. Many school yards are filled with tomorrow's superstars of RPS, and this early sparring is critical to their future in the sport. More formalized training for children is available through the Junior RPS-sters of the World RPS Society, but the entrance exams and annual fees are not within the reach of many young players and their families. Educators and child-care workers have long understood the benefits of stopping an argument quickly by settling the matter with RPS.

Casual Play

Not all RPS clubs need to be so formalized. Groups of friends can create their own ad hoc clubs as a way to re-solve everyday disputes or in order to meet infrequently for a match or two. The player who masters many of the techniques and strategies in this book will find his qual-ity of life considerably improved through winning more often at RPS. Situations for using RPS appear con-stantly. We list a few common situations below.

Domestic RPS

Fraternity members and groups of friends living to-gether often waste considerable time debating matters such as who must get off the couch to supply the group with beer or who must answer the telephone when it rings. Adopting RPS as the default dispute-resolution de-vice can streamline the process considerably. Instead of arguing over whose turn it is to pick up snacks for Sun-day afternoon football or some other chore, all one per-son must do is stick out his fist as a way to call for a game. The same is true of the frequent squabbles of spouses or families. Taking the garbage out, walking the dog, and changing diapers are frequent sources of fric-tion that use of RPS can alleviate.

Paying the Bill with RPS

Should you find yourself going for a night on the town with a group of friends, try using RPS as a way to determine who buys the next round of drinks or who pays for dinner. Playing well in these situations will pay for the price of this book many times over.

RPS at the Office

Many progressive managers bring RPS into the workplace as an unbiased way to distribute workload, award promotions, and assign overtime or company picnic responsibilities. It cannot be overemphasized that playing RPS well in these situations is critical to maintaining personal job satisfaction and limiting your stress level.

Now that the club is established, a great way to jump-start the first meeting is to invite a well-known local RPS player to speak and to offer tips and inspiration. Despite the demands of the pro circuit, many leading players generously offer their time to speak at smaller RPS clubs. With the exception of a few egotistical professional RPS players, speaking fees are usually surprisingly affordable.

Training exercises and scrimmages are important, but members of the club have likely joined with a desire to vie for supremacy in the RPS arena. The main goals of any RPS club should be to organize an active league or tournament and to provide players with the practical skills they need to compete.

BECOMING A CHAPTER OF THE WORLD RPS SOCIETY

If your club is growing and successful, consider applying for membership as an official chapter of the World RPS Society. Clubs accepted for inclusion with the society will adhere to the following guidelines:

- The club cannot exclude anyone based on immaterial factors such as race, gender, physical or mental handicap, or perceived nerdiness.
- All members must become card-carrying members of the World RPS Society.
- The club must have a distinct name that is not shared by another official club nor is intentional misspelling for comedic effect permitted (e.g., Sizzor Boyz)
- The club must play and hold regular tournaments using the official World RPS Society Rules of Play.
- The club must seek to develop and field players for local and regional tournaments.

Visit worldrps.com for more details on gaining official club status and to download a club application form.

RUNNING A TOURNAMENT

The type of thick-witted soul who believes that RPS is a simple game is also likely to harbor another falsehood:

that setting up an RPS tournament is uncomplicated. There are many factors to consider when setting up a tournament. Whether one is an experienced RPS tournament organizer or looking to fulfill a lifelong dream of becoming one, this guide has been written to help. The main reasons for holding a tournament are making a profit, fund-raising, corporate team-building, or just plain having fun.

TOURNAMENT FORMATS

Single Elimination

This is the easiest type of tournament to organize. Each player plays one other player, with the winner moving forward to the next round and the loser being eliminated from play. For a given number of competitors, a single-elimination tournament takes the least amount of time to complete. Single elimination requires the organizer to keep track of only the winners.

The main drawback with this style is that players who lose a match at any time will be removed from the game. Half of the total people in the tournament will be eliminated in the first round of the game. Due to the simplicity of setup, this format is best for larger tournaments involving 128 or more players. While attracting more than one hundred players may seem like a stretch for a fledgling club, it is wise to prepare for a runaway

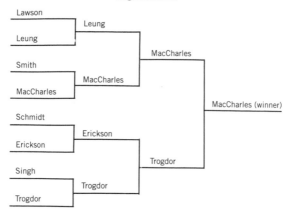

Single Elimination

Lawson

Leung

Leung

    MacCharles

Smith

MacCharles

MacCharles

                  MacCharles (winner)

Schmidt

Erickson

Erickson

    Trogdor

Singh

Trogdor

Trogdor

success. Make sure to speak personally with the disappointed first-time players and inform them that they made the wrong choice of throw and have no one to blame but themselves. Then quickly recruit them into the club, describing it as a way they can sharpen their obviously deficient skills.

Double Elimination

This format is a bit more complicated and requires additional setup and monitoring of the process. Each player is guaranteed to play in at least two matches. All players are entered into the primary bracket. After each match, the loser of the round is given a second chance and moved down to the secondary bracket. In the second and later rounds, losers from the primary bracket move to

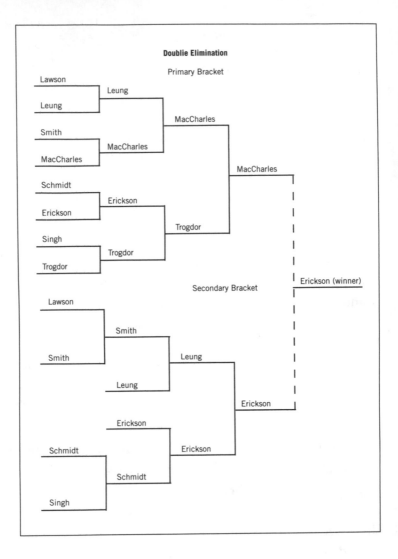

Doublie Elimination

Primary Bracket

Lawson
Leung
Leung

Smith
MacCharles
MacCharles

Schmidt
Erickson
Erickson

Singh
Trogdor
Trogdor

MacCharles

Trogdor

MacCharles

Erickson (winner)

Secondary Bracket

Lawson

Smith
Smith

Leung

Leung

Schmidt

Erickson
Erickson

Singh
Schmidt

Erickson

the corresponding round on the secondary bracket. When players lose while on the secondary bracket, they are eliminated from the tournament. Rounds continue until both the primary and secondary brackets have a winner, and then a final takes place. Some organizers avoid this type of tournament, not only because of the complexity, but also because the notion of giving a second chance to a player who has lost a match offends many RPS purists.

Round Robin

In this format, each competitor plays against every other competitor, thus providing each player with many opportunities to compete. Win and loss records are kept for each player. The championship round is made up of those players in the top 50 percentile, based upon their win-loss ratio. Round-robin formats are very well suited to league play for smaller clubs and tournaments. Beginners enjoy this style of tournament since they are given the freedom to fail over and over again before finally being eliminated from play. This is by far the most complex format to manage and is not recommended for tournaments involving a great number of competitors.

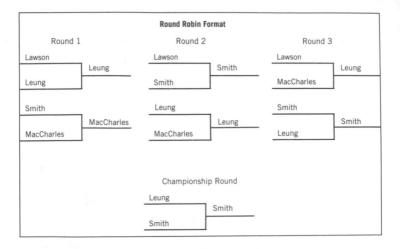

Round Robin Format

Round 1	Round 2	Round 3
Lawson	Lawson	Lawson
Leung	Smith	Leung
Leung	Smith	MacCharles
Smith	Leung	Smith
MacCharles	Leung	Smith
MacCharles	MacCharles	Leung

Championship Round

Leung
Smith
Smith

Championship Format—
Octagonal Ladder with Single Elimination

At the World Championships, players are assigned to one of several qualifying arenas in groups of eight. Single elimination is used for each group until only two players from each group remain. The two players are then each placed into separate groups for the second round. This system repeats with winners grouped into eights and the two winning players moving forward until there are only sixteen players. The final sixteen players then play single elimination for the final-stage matches.

In order to ensure that a single winner remains at the end of the World Championship, the World RPS Society uses a preset number of participants. These numbers work in such a way that they guarantee a situation with a single

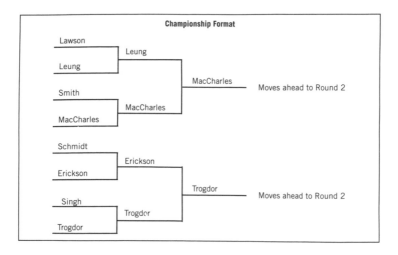

Championship Format

Lawson

Leung

Leung

Leung

MacCharles

Moves ahead to Round 2

Smith

MacCharles

MacCharles

Schmidt

Erickson

Erickson

Erickson

Trogdor

Moves ahead to Round 2

Singh

Trogdor

Trogdor

Trogdor

winner and with no byes or defaults required. These numbers are the various exponents of two (or 2^n). Tournaments of exactly 2, 4, 8, 16, 32, 64, 128, 256 or 512 participants will all condense neatly down to a final match, provided all players are available at their starting times.

Random Distribution and Seeding

Most regional and smaller tournaments use random seeding, where competitors are randomly assigned their matches and arenas. This is often accomplished by the order in which players register by handing each competitor a card or competition bib with a number on it.

Seeded tournaments require preestablished ranks for the competitors. The various brackets are then balanced to keep players playing within their skill level.

This usually requires some type of qualifying round or even a full season to lead up to a seeded-playoff scenario.

Byes

There is nothing more vexing for an organizer than having an insufficient number of players materialize for a well-publicized tournament or having a player who does not appear at his assigned time. This is when byes must be used. A bye is the right for a competitor to proceed uncontested into the next round. Byes are awarded by the referee and in some cases must be approved by the tournament grand marshal.

Sanctioned vs. Unsanctioned Tournaments

A sanctioned tournament is one that is run according to the World RPS Society tournament standards. Obtaining the rights to a sanctioned tournament can be a rigorous process. We outline the major criteria below:

- ★ *All referees have received adequate training from an accredited World RPS Society training official.*
- ★ *Tournament proceedings must be supervised by an authorized World RPS Society official.*
- ★ *Tournament organizer has provided an approved tournament proposal to World RPS Society and paid any necessary fees.*

To obtain approval for a tournament, please contact the World RPS Society for all the details. Many tournaments are refused sanctioning every year, for not adhering to tournament standards and protocol. Make sure the plan adheres to the necessary guidelines.

Sponsorship

Sponsorship of RPS tournaments is not what it once was. Glove manufacturers, paper mills, mining companies, and surgical-instruments manufacturers have all curtailed spending in recent years. Combine this with new tournaments cropping up, and finding the necessary funds to host a high-quality tournament becomes more difficult for the aspiring tournament organizer. Local small merchants or larger multinational mega-corporations can often be a good source of sponsorship funds.

Venue Selection

The best possible place for a tournament, league, or club meeting is a large indoor open area free from distractions. Gymnasiums, large basements, studios, church social areas, legion halls, and even nightclubs (when not in use) are all excellent choices. Where there is a choice, err on the side of more space rather than less, so that several matches may go on simultaneously. The extra space will also allow spectators, coaches, and trainers ample room to view the action from various angles while limiting chance collisions and injuries. Playing outdoors can be a nice change of pace for experienced players; however, many new players are distracted by the noise, bright sunshine, curious spectators, and indigenous flora and fauna.

Qualifying Arenas

If the tournament is larger than sixteen players, multiple qualifying arenas will probably be necessary. Each arena should be a sectioned-off area in order to keep the usual teeming crowds back from the site. Clearly name or

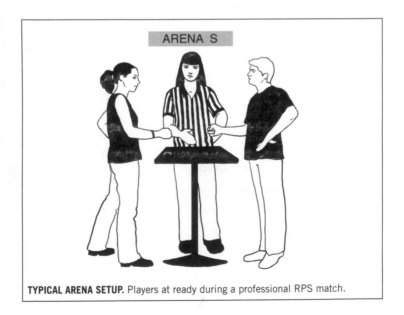

TYPICAL ARENA SETUP. Players at ready during a professional RPS match.

number the arenas to ensure that players can easily find their play location. Most professional-level arenas provide a small table between the players as a physical barrier. For an official arena, the distance between the players should be no less than one cubit and no more than two cubits (a cubit is the distance between elbow and fingertips). Referees are responsible for keeping a clean arena and ensuring a good flow between games.

Extra Equipment

The following equipment, although not strictly necessary, can be helpful for tournaments and clubs:

Chalkboard—for scorekeeping or strategy lessons

Various color-coded name tags—for identifying players and classifying skill levels into beginner, rookie, novice, advanced, expert, and master

Masking tape—for marking out playing areas

A whistle or megaphone—for commanding attention

Gold stars or similar stickers—for signifying distinction in competition or novel strategic plays during practice

Throw signs—Two each for Rock, Paper, and Scissors are held up by volunteers so that spectators at the back can tell what throws have been made. At larger tournaments it is customary for the throw signs to be brandished on the main stage by attractive young women in tight clothing.

Officiating

Unless the event is a large sanctioned tournament, it may be difficult to find accredited referees, due a serious backlog at the RPS Training Center. Sanctioned referees have to complete a rigorous accreditation program that can often require years of preparation, internship, and testing. Sometimes an organizer can get lucky since many apprentice referees will plod through the lower-ranked tournament circuit searching to earn enough hours to gain their full accreditation. Keep an eye out in Internet RPS chat groups for referees looking to earn their hours.

If accredited referees are difficult to find, training new ones is your best option. Do not underestimate the importance of providing a comprehensive training program. There is nothing more frustrating for players than to have a referee who does not have a firm grasp of the rules. Often the best refs are the people who secretly yearn for more respect and power, so try these people first; they will relish the opportunity. Frequently, failed former players become the most feared referees. A passion for the sport combined with wretched performance on the pro circuit eventually evolves into a complete intolerance for slipshod form and a genuine animosity toward competitors.

Referees must keep abreast of the latest Official

Rules of the Grand Sport of Rock Paper Scissors and must understand not only the language but also the spirit of the rules. Unique situations will always arise in RPS, and if the referee grasps the spirit of the rules, he will be able to make the right call.

KEEPING SCORE

Because most tournaments use multiple-throw formats (i.e., best of three of three) rather than lightning rounds, a ref's most obvious responsibility is to keep the score of the two players straight. A ref will lose all credibility if he needs to ask the players about the score. Referees should use an official score sheet or develop a reliable finger-counting method.

DEALING WITH FOULS

Another important part of the referee's job is to deal with infraction situations. Referees have complete authority in awarding penalties. This is the art of refereeing and how they choose to mete out justice through penalties is how professional referees are measured. What follows is a list of the potential calls and their recommended outcomes:

1. **Primes not in synch.** Referee should immediately stop play (preferably before the players have committed to their final approach) and call a do over. A firm word directed at both players to get in synch is usually all that is needed to get the players to conform.

2. **Illegal throw.** Automatic disqualification. A referee must understand that the very integrity of the game is at risk if he allows a stray Dynamite or Texas Longhorn into the match without penalty. Any player using a throw outside of the trinity should be made to suffer an immediate match loss and shameful ejection from the arena. Some bleeding-heart refs prefer to provide only the penalty of a point loss, depending upon the circumstances, but this is rare, considering the severity of the offense.

3. **Questionable throws.** Questionable throws are any improper hand positions or indecisive throws. The difference between an illegal throw and a questionable throw often boils down to the player's intent. If a ref believes that an error was made out of inexperience or ignorance, he may choose to issue a warning. A good example of this is the use of Vertical Paper. If the player is nervous and the ref understands that the player simply made a rookie error, he may let it slide with a simple warning. A good ref will not offer more than one warning, otherwise he risks losing the respect of the opposing player.

4. **Stalemate.** Should players come out with the same throw, the ref simply needs to ask the players to replay the point until a decisive win is achieved.

5. **Player contact.** RPS is a noncontact sport, and therefore players have no need for direct knuckle-on-knuckle contact. Again, this boils down to intent. Should the contact be incidental, refs should simply issue a warning to both

Player on left attempts to rattle his opponent but only forces a stalemate. Player on right vents frustration. (Photo by Mark Coatsworth)

players. At other times, one player is seeking to bully the other as a momentum-shifting tactic. Referees should be firm in these situations and issue a loss of match to any player maliciously coming into contact with another player's fist or arm.

6. **Obnoxious behavior.** There is a fine line between athletic bravado/posturing and truly obnoxious behavior. A ref needs to assess each situation individually, with an eye toward behavior displaying blatant disrespect for the game, the opponent, the referee, or the World RPS Society. A ref may let two rival players "go at each other" as long as he knows that both players are willing participants. Referees should have a low tolerance for direct verbal assaults (es-

pecially against the ref himself). The ref has the discretion to choose between issuing a warning, imposing a loss of point, or imposing a loss of match, depending on the severity of situation.

It is important to note that all referee decisions are final and cannot be overturned by the grand marshal, the tournament organizer, or any other interested party. Furthermore, there is *no* appeal process. RPS referees enjoy an authority unmatched by other sports officials. This may help to explain why players in the know treat referees with such immense respect and awe.

REFEREE'S CREDO

I shall always:

- Retain the highest reverence for the sport of RPS
- Preserve the poise of my rank and responsibility
- Sustain a professional division from both players and coaches
- Remain faithful to my brother and sister officials, and neither permit nor promote criticism of them
- Organize the players effectively by being polite and considerate without sacrificing firmness
- Consider it a privilege to be a member of the WRPSS and uphold its ideals at all times
- Know that I cannot allow personal relationships to affect my professional standards
- Support the notion that the ideal official sees all, but is seldom noticed

---

How to Be a Good Ref

A good ref will seek to be invisible in order to let the players play their game. A good ref is decisive yet fair. A good ref is respected, not loved.

FLOW

Refs have a responsibility to the organizer to ensure the game stays on schedule. Tournament refs have dozens of games to play and must keep their games moving forward. Players who take too long in between games or request too many time-outs should be given firm warnings. The referee should use these moments to assert authority and help establish credibility with the players. A ref can also change the flow of the game to help the players out of a difficult situation. For example, if too many stalemates occur in a row during a heated match, consider asking the players to take a breather to collect their thoughts and rethink their game strategy. A short break is often all that is needed to get the players' heads straight and back into the game.

APPROACH: The downward stroke of the final prime prior to the delivery phase.

BEST THREE OF THREE: Style of play in which a player must win two best-of-three sets to win the match. Usual format for pro tournaments.

BEST THREE OF FIVE: Style of play in which a player must win three best-of-three sets to win the match. Usual format for pro tournament finals.

BULL BOARD: The World RPS Society online Bulletin Board (www.worldrps.com) gets its name from the frequent lies or "bull" that appears when players speak of their prowess at the game.

CHAOS PLAY: A highly skilled RPS strategy where the player attempts to make their throw pattern so complex that it is unpredictable by another opponent.

CLOAKING: The act of disguising a throw of Paper or Scissors as a Rock during the approach phase until the last possible moment.

CORPORAL PUNISHMENT RPS: A violent and unsanctioned version of play that results in pain inflicted upon the loser of a match by the winner.

CUBIT: A standard unit of length used in RPS. Technically the distance is defined as the distance between tip of middle finger and forearm.

DELIVERY: The phase of the game when a player's hand transitions from the priming position to a throw position of Rock, Paper, or Scissors.

FEED THE PONY: An alternative to the traditional palm-down delivery of Paper; in this case, Paper is delivered with the palm facing upward. Feed the Pony is considered acceptable form since it includes the necessary 90-degree wrist rotation.

FORCED ROCK: Any throw delivered too late during the delivery phase (i.e., past the 90-degree cutoff) must be considered a Rock by the presiding official.

GAMBIT: A series of three throws made with strategic intent.

GAMESMANSHIP: This term was coined by Author Stephen Potter, who defined it as "the art of winning without actually cheating."

GLOSSARY: An alphabetical sorting of technical RPS words along with their definitions.

HONOR: An essential component of RPS. An unfailing commitment to adhere to any decision reached via an RPS match. Alternately a reference to a player's honor standing when playing for honor, as opposed to making a decision.

ILLEGAL THROW: Any throw which is not Rock, Paper or Scissors.

JANKEN: One of many alternate names for the game of RPS. The game is referred to as Janken, or Jan Ken Pon, in Japan.

LEGAL THROW: Rock, Paper, or Scissors.

META-STRATEGY: Any strategy that is not part of the actual game itself, often taking the form of misleading an opponent into a rash throw or false prediction. Also known as Gamesmanship.

MIRROR PLAY: When players deliver strategies resulting in identical throws. In essence a repetitive series of stalemates or ties.

PAPER: One of the basic elements of RPS. Paper beats Rock and is beaten in turn by Scissors.

PAPER CLIPPING: Any of a group of meta-strategies that attempt to force an opponent into a play of Paper.

PRIME: The act of retracting one's fist from full extension of the arm toward the shoulder multiple times prior to the approach phase of the game in order to synchronize players' delivery of throws.

RANDOMNESS: An unfounded belief that RPS players are capable of completely unpredictable sequences of throws. Not to be confused with Chaos play.

ROCK: One of the basic elements of RPS. Rock beats Scissors and is beaten in turn by Paper.

ROSHAMBO: Another of the many names for the sport of RPS that are frequently encountered in the United States.

SCRIPTERS: A general term for players who prefer to plan their strategies well before a tournament.

SCISSORS: One of the basic elements of RPS. Scissors beats Paper and is beaten in turn by Rock.

STALEMATE: When two players have played identical throws resulting in a tie.

STREET RPS: Unsanctioned gambling matches outside of tournaments or clubs.

TELLS: Physical signals that betray a player's next throw.

TRINITY: Short-hand reference to the three throws of Rock, Paper, or Scissors. Sometimes called the noble throws.

THREE-PRIME SHOOT: The act of priming three times prior to delivering a throw. Also known as International Standard Priming Convention or European Rules.

TRINITY SQUARE PLAZA: The headquarters of the World RPS Society in Toronto, Ontario.

TWO-PRIME SHOOT: The act of priming only two times prior to delivering a throw. Also known as North American Rules.

VERTICAL PAPER: Paper delivered with palm flat, but not perpendicular to the floor. Widely considered bad form and frequently penalized during tournament play.

ZONE PLAY: The exhilarating experience of being at one with the game to the point that the game becomes effortless. While in the zone a player can usually see an opponent's next several moves with absolute clarity. Similar to what Buddhists refer to as "Nirvana."

APPENDIX 1

THE OFFICIAL RULES OF
THE GRAND SPORT OF
ROCK PAPER SCISSORS

BACKGROUND

These general rules apply to all Rock Paper Scissors (RPS) matches, its tripartite variants known in any permutation and/or combination of the following Scissors, Paper, Rock/Stone and by any other name that is currently known or unknown to the World RPS Society, including Roshambo, Janken, or Jan Ken Po.

DEFINITION

RPS is a decision-making game of wits, speed, dexterity, and strategy between players who are unable to reach a decision using other means. The result of a match is considered a binding agreement between the players. In the case of professional or tournament play, the decision is replaced by honor points toward a championship title. RPS is a game played by honorable people and therefore every effort should be made to commit to the outcome. The game is played by substituting the elements of Rock, Paper, and Scissors with standard hand signals.

RULE GOVERNANCE

These rules are governed, maintained, published, updated, authorized, and approved by the World RPS Society under the guidance and authority of the World RPS Steering Committee. Any changes are in strict violation of the World RPS Society's Responsibility Code. Any changes to the rules require a seven-eighths majority ruling by the World RPS Steering Committee, unless a temporary waiving of or amendment to is agreed upon by the players prior to commencing play (no temporary waiving of rules are permitted for championship matches). All temporary amendments are considered ephemeral unless otherwise agreed upon, but they must not include any variant throws beyond the basic trinity such as, but not limited to, Dynamite, Bird, Well, Spock, God, Water, Lightning, Bomb, Matchstick, and/or Texas Longhorn.

THE SETUP

1.0 Prior to play commencing, the players must agree upon what decision is to be made (and considered binding) as a result of the match. If nothing can be agreed upon and the players wish to continue play, the match automatically defaults to an "honor" match. This is the case for tournaments, festivals, and championship matches.

1.1 Players must agree to the number of primes to be used prior to the approach. Two and three primes are most commonly used in professional-level play. The three-prime shoot is required for championship matches.

1.1.1 The decision makers must stand opposite each other with one outstretched fist at waist height with a distance between their fists of no less than 1 cubit and no more than 2 cubits.

1.2 The players also must establish the number of games and sets to be played before the match is concluded. If no agreement can be reached, the match defaults to a best-of-three-games format. Qualifying rounds for the World Championships use the best-of-three-of-three format (best of three games = one set, best of three sets = the match). Semifinals and the final match use a best-of-three-of-five format (best of thee games = one set, best of five sets = the match).

2.0 A "call for prime" is issued by one player (or the referee) to his/her opponent(s) in a recognizable audible tone (RAT).

2.1 A RAT is defined as an utterance that can be heard by the opponent and/or referee. Using the word "ready" is considered standard form.

2.1.1 In the case of a match between or with hearing-impaired players or in situations where it is critical that silence be maintained, a mutually agreed upon recognizable visual signal (RVS) can replace the standard RAT. In this case, a nod of the head while looking directly into the eyes of the other player is considered standard form.

2.2 A "return of the call" is then issued by the opposing player who thus acknowledges the "call for prime," also in a RAT or RVS.

2.3 Once the "return of the call" has been established, players are considered to be "at ready."

2.3.1 Play may commence anytime after the players are established and recognized as being "at ready."

2.4 The game is considered to be "in play" after any player "breaks ready" and thus "initiates the prime."

PRIMING

3.0 The vertical prime is performed by retracting the outstretched fist back toward the player's shoulder (players must face each other and perform the prime with arms parallel). The vertical prime is required for championship matches.

3.0.1 The fist should be retracted toward the player's own body rather than his opponent's to avoid possible contact. Contact between players during a tournament may result in faults and/or disqualification at the discretion of the referee presiding.

3.1 As soon as one player has "broken ready" and initiated the first prime, it is the responsibility and obligation of the opponent also to begin priming and to "catch" or "synch" the prime so the players can establish an approach and delivery in unison.

3.1.1 The player who has initiated the prime is under the strict obligation to maintain a constant priming speed so as to give his opponent every opportunity to "catch the prime."

3.2 The fist must remain in the closed position until the delivery of the final prime. The fist is the only acceptable hand position during the prime.

3.2.1 The fist must remain in full view of the opposing player and may not come in contact with any outside influences that inhibit the opponent's view.

3.2.2 One or both players may, at their own discretion, opt to use their nonpriming hand held flat with palm upward as a "level gauge" or "platform." This is sometimes referred to as "one hand clapping" and is used to ensure the player does not prime past 90-degrees.

3.3 Prior to the delivery of the final prime, the game may be called off only for the following reasons: rule clarification, decision clarification, or injury.

APPROACH

4.0 Once the fist has reached the highest point of the final throw of the last prime, the delivery of the throw is considered to be "in approach." At any time during the approach of this final prime, the hand may be released in any of the following manners:

Rock: Is represented by a closed fist with the thumb resting at least at the same height as the topmost finger of the hand. The thumb must not be concealed by the fingers. Note: To accommodate different throwing styles, it is considered legal for the tip of the thumb to point downward.

Scissors: Is delivered in the same manner as Rock with the exception that the index and middle fingers are fully extended toward the opposing player. It is considered good form to angle the topmost finger upward and the lower finger downward in order to create a roughly 30 to 45 degree angle between the two digits and thus mimic a pair of scissors. (Wiggling fingers in a scissorlike motion or making "snipping" sounds is considered bad form.)

Paper: Is delivered in the same manner as Rock with the exception that all fingers including the thumb are fully extended and horizontal, with the points of the fingers facing the opposing player. Use of the Vertical Paper (sometimes referred to as the "handshake") is considered exceptionally bad form. Throws must be delivered prior to the completion of the approach.

4.1 The approach is considered complete when the forearm is at a 90-degree angle to the upper body. Any throw not delivered prior to the hand crossing the 90-degree mark shall be considered a throw of Rock. Use of throws other than Rock, Paper, and Scissors in a championship match is grounds for disqualification.

Delivery

5.0 Participants must exercise extreme dexterity, caution, and care to not initiate contact between the opposing fists during any point of the priming phase. The direct contact of the fists can cause scraping, chaffing, or rapping of the knuckles. Make sure any onlookers are aware of the intentions of the players as the swinging of closed fists can be mistaken as a sign of a potentially combative situation.

5.0.1 Should direct contact occur, players should stop play immediately and assess any personal injuries before restarting the prime and replaying the game.

5.1 After players have revealed their throws, play must stop until an agreement can be reached as to the winner or whether a stalemate situation has arisen.

Throws

6.0 Player has the full range of throws to play, as follows:

    6.0.1 Rock: wins against Scissors, loses to Paper, stalemates against itself.

    6.0.2 Paper: wins against Rock, loses to Scissors, stalemates against itself.

    6.0.3 Scissors: wins against Paper, loses to Rock, stalemates against itself.

6.1 Players may use any combination of these throws at any time throughout the match. Any throw that does not conform to the standard hand positions (outlined above) shall be considered to be an illegal throw and is thus forbidden in tournament play. Should a player execute an illegal throw, the opposing player has the right (but not the obligation) to claim immediate victory over the match. Alternatively, the infringed-upon player has the right (but not the obligation) to replay the current game if he so chooses. In championship play, the offending player may be disqualified or the game replayed at the sole discretion of the presiding official.

6.2 The winner of the game is dictated by the player's throw which beats that of the opponent's throw. Under no circumstances can a losing throw ever beat a winning throw, nor may an illegal throw beat a legal throw.

6.3 In the case of a stalemate, in which players reveal the same throw, the game must be replayed. There are no limits to the number of stalemates that may occur in any given match. Should players find themselves in a continuous stalemate situation, also known as "Mirror Play," a good approach is to take a short "time-out" to rethink strategy.

Postgame Play

7.0 There is no limit to the number of games, sets, or matches that can be played in RPS. The games may continue until any and all decisions are reached at the discretion of the players involved. Matches for honor can be substituted at any point after the conclusion of a match if agreed upon by all players involved before the beginning of the next match. Championship matches are mandated as a best-of-three-of-three format, with the option of best-of-three-of-five matches for the semifinal and final rounds.

Note: At the conclusion of the match, after the winner has been determined, some players will offer a Vertical Paper throw, or handshake. While in other circles it is considered good manners to thank your opponent for a match in this way, this action should not be expected or required in RPS. In general, a handshake is used as "deal sealer" between two parties. Since the results of an RPS match are considered to be binding, the handshake is considered a redundancy, in effect, the "deal" has already been "sealed" with the outcome of the match.

DISCLAIMER

The World RPS Society does not take any responsibility, legal or otherwise, as a result of any actions or inactions performed as a result of a decision made or changed via the use of the game. In addition, the World RPS Society does not govern, manage, police, or endorse any nonhonor activity resulting from a decision made via RPS. It is the sole responsibility of the players involved to govern the outcomes of any matches. The World RPS Society does not encourage, endorse, or promote the use of RPS in illegal, immoral, and/or life-threatening situations. RPS should be used only in situations in which the two parties cannot reach agreement via other means, in competitive play, or in order to make the decision-making process more enjoyable. Offering to use RPS to determine an outcome of a previously decided upon event is in strict violation of the World RPS Society's Players Responsibility Code and will not be considered binding even if one of the players was unaware of the previous decision. All players assume any and all risks associated with playing the sport. It is not recommended that novices attempt to use the physical versions of the RPS elements because they can cause serious harm or injury if not played properly.

If any further information is required, please consult the World RPS Society's pamphlet "It's Your Life: When Not to Use RPS as a Decision-Making vehicle."

These rules are considered full and complete and cannot be deviated from or altered unless specifically noted to the contrary in the game rules.

MEMBERSHIP IN
THE WORLD RPS SOCIETY

Interested in RPS? Looking for others who are, too?

The World RPS Society is an international organization for RPS players, and we are looking for people like you!

You can become a member of this exciting organization! When joining, you will receive:

★ *An official World RPS Society membership card, allowing you to declare your active status in the World RPS Society*

★ *A letter of welcome, signed by the legendary Wojek Smallsoa (including an excerpt from his seminal work,* The Trio of Hands*)*

★ *Your very own official title in the World RPS Society proclaimed boldly on your card*

★ *A sticker featuring one of the designs from the World RPS Historical Archive*

PLUS . . .

Written on the back of the card is a special bonus available only to card-bearing World RPS Society members. Showing your card at the beginning of any match with a nonmember will enable you to dictate the number of rounds to be played! So any time you play a nonmember, you can force your opponent to play a number of rounds that suits your best playing strategies.

For more information visit www.worldrps.com.

ACKNOWLEDGMENTS

Rebuilding the society to its former glory is not a task that can be accomplished by two people alone. Many people actively participate, support, and promote the World RPS Society and our goals.

This book would never have happened without the foresight of our agent Laurie Abkemeier, to whom we are greatly indebted. Our editor at Fireside, Amanda Patten, must be recognized for her courageous and enthusiastic support and input on this project. Our illustrator Megan Bannon worked tirelessly under tight deadlines to meet our requests. We would also like to thank the inimitable Bull Boarder arbiter for his extraordinary work on advanced RPS theory and strategy, as well as Benjamin Peterson for critical Japanese translations. Design work on charts was generously donated by Karen Walker.

The members of the society and the World RPS Bull Board, particularly Custardchuk, Fisted Sophist, Garth Breaks, Rockefeller, and Al Thorn, among many others, have made innumerable contributions to the organization and the game. The multitalented C. Urbanus has been a constant source of dry wit, support, and friendship for many years. Master Roshambollah has been the society's most famous (and frequently infamous) ambassador, traveling across the world to compete and promote the goals of the society. The worldrps.com art direction by Michael Halminen and design work by Rob Ciancamerla has been invaluable to the site's success. Naomi, Tod, and Justice Brilliant were wonderful hosts at the Roshambo Wineries in Healdsburg, California, where they provide the finest Dry Creek zinfandel in copious amounts.

The World Championships have been made possible largely by the superhuman efforts of Michael Booth in his role as host/producer, along with Pete Kaulbach as grand marshal. Our referees are too numerous to list, but we thank each and every one of you for your time, dedication to the cause, and sound judgment. However, for consistent year-over-year adjudication, Brent Andruko, Colin Ballantyne, and the most feared official on the circuit—Elizabeth Bromstein—must be mentioned. Benjamin Stein and the crew at AllTooFlat.com must be thanked for photos and attending the yearly championships. Mike Vanaselja has been of great help in chronicling the events. Lawrence Partington led the way through the world of television production and helped to take the championships to new heights. The championships would not have been possible without the legal assistance of Derrick Chua and the following event volunteers: Keri Alletson, Greg Cooke, Jennifer Ballantyne, Andrea Polackova, Jan Dunnel, Laura Bell, Michelle Michalak, Lisa Naccarato, and Justine Poole, along with Andrea and Jason Krawchuk. Congratulations to Pete Lovering and Rob Krueger for representing the sport and the society as true champions. We also wish to thank all of the international competitors, spectators, and media for your enthusiastic support of the Rock Paper Scissors World Championships. In particular, journalists Paul Cabana and Ken Hegan wrote compelling accounts of the sport of RPS, which catapulted us to a higher altitude.

The authors also wish to thank Fipi Lele for her support and constant inspiration. Jayne Mitchell is largely responsible for our involvement with the society, by introducing us to the work of Stephen Potter. We thank Ross and Audrey Walker for being great and understanding parents, but mostly for keeping their opinions of our endeavors to themselves. We appreciate our aunt Clara for her diligent media clipping expertise. For infinite patience, public-relations skill, inspiration, and first-round editing Lisa Walker deserves immense gratitude.

    ACKNOWLEDGMENTS